T0194962

JUST FOLLOW JESUS

What Jesus Means When He Calls

Billy Joseph Stines

WESTBOW
P R E S S®
A DIVISION OF THOMAS NELSON
& ZONDERVAN

WestBow Press books may be ordered through booksellers or by contacting:

WestBow Press
A Division of Thomas Nelson & Zondervan
1663 Liberty Drive
Bloomington, IN 47403
www.westbowpress.com
1 (866) 928-1240

ISBN: 978-1-9736-8190-8 (sc)
ISBN: 978-1-9736-8192-2 (hc)
ISBN: 978-1-9736-8191-5 (e)

Library of Congress Control Number: 2019920669

Print information available on the last page.

WestBow Press rev. date: 12/10/2019

This book is dedicated

to

the Lord Jesus Christ

and my wife

for all her support and encouragement

down through the years.

Contents

For God has not given us a spirit of fear, but one of power, love, and sound judgment. So don't be ashamed of the testimony about our Lord, or of me his prisoner. Instead, share the suffering for the gospel, relying on the power of God. He has saved us and called us with a holy calling, not according to our works, but according to his own purpose and grace which was given to us in Christ Jesus before time began. (2 Timothy 1:7–9)

Be diligent to present yourself to God as one approved, a worker who doesn't need to be ashamed, correctly teaching the word of truth. (2 Timothy 2:15)

I solemnly charge you before God and Christ Jesus, who is going to judge the living and dead, and because of his appearing and his kingdom: Preach the word; be ready in season and out of season; rebuke, correct, and encourage with great patience and teaching. (2 Timothy 4:1–2)

Introduction

A number of years ago I was teaching on Jesus's parable of the sower[1] when one of the pillars of the church challenged my interpretation. I had simply stated what had become so obvious to my simple mind during my study of the passage—that each person had heard the Word, and each had responded to that Word in some way. The first individuals reject the word together, while the next two groups had wandered away after a time—from the cause of Christ, maybe never to return—the first due to persecution and the second because of the cares of the world. In contrast, the fourth group heard the Word of God and produced fruit—"some a hundred, some sixty, some thirty times what was sown"—thereby showing themselves to be his disciples.[2] Although he struggled to defend his point of view, this deacon and Sunday school teacher took great exception with the suggestion that the second and third group may have turned their backs on Christ; therefore, may not be numbered among Christ's true followers. The truth is that he was only giving voice to what had become a common teaching in the church—that once we are saved, we are always saved no matter what may be the true nature of our relationship with the Lord Jesus Christ, if any at all.

While I also believe that once we are saved, we are always saved, it bothers me that our reasoning may ignore all sides of the issue. Apparently, many have very little understanding of what the Bible actually says. Instead they focus upon those portions of God's Word that support their ideas and make them feel good, while dismissing those parts that do not fit into their idea of who God is. Sadly, it is our tendency to seek peace through compromise rather than striving to discover the Truth—Jesus Christ. My friend, this is the spiritual issue that we must wrestle with in our society. How do we call people to God when the world is drawing them away from him? And how to we get them to understand the true nature of his great love? This means we must also wrestle with the implications of God's judgment and how it relates to the message of the New Testament regarding love, mercy, and grace. Furthermore, are we living in true Christian love when we completely ignore the disturbing warnings spoken through divine-selected writers to a corrupt godless society? Do the admonishments found in the Bible still apply to the day in which we live? And if they do—how?

Anyone who claims Jesus Christ as Savior and Lord should wrestle with these issues. The ramifications are too far-reaching and too important to be ignored or be settled quickly by God-fearing people. Too often, instead of struggling with the full implicates of scripture, we take the easy route and base our explanations upon human reasoning laced with human emotion. When we choose the easy way out, we should ask ourselves other questions. Is our faith in something other than in Jesus Christ? Where is the influence of the God's Spirit in the whole process? What does this say about the place of God's Word in our lives? Can we even be considered followers of Jesus if he is left completely out of our daily lives?

It seems to me that for most of us the simplest interpretation of scripture is usually the best interpretation. We should never twist the plain truth of scripture to remove the spiritual tension created by the Lord's teaching. After all, Jesus never sugarcoated his teachings to gain followers. This implies that we must endeavor to permit the Bible to speak for itself and not allow public opinion to contaminate our understanding of what the Master is saying through his written word. It also means taking God at his word and accepting certain portions of scripture as a mystery of God that is beyond our understanding at this point in our spiritual journey. The simple truth is that no one has all the answers except Jesus Christ. To explain away what different passages are literally saying without a good biblical reason is dangerous for Christianity. Moreover, to water down the difficult passages to ease our consciences does not glorify Christ and may mislead people regarding their relationship to Jesus Christ.

Lately a deeply troubled spirit has developed within me, particularly as I read the Bible against the backdrop of the society in which we live. Two questions are constantly on my mind. First, am I being true to the LORD God in my interpretation of scripture? Through much Bible study and prayer, as well as reading the thoughts of others more knowledgeable and spiritual individuals, I seek daily to remain true to my Lord. Through his Spirit, God has often worked to correct my misinterpretation of the Bible. But my greatest struggle is with the second question. By our silence, to not sound judgmental, are we allowing people—people we love dearly— to face God's judgment unprepared? This seems to be the more difficult question to answer. How do we declare the truths of the Bible and at the same time act as a conduit for God's unconditional love and boundless grace?

The reality is that we need this tension in our lives to keep us constantly dependent upon the Holy Spirit in all areas of our lives. This is not to set aside our deep convictions regarding Jesus Christ, but it is to recognize that such a strain motivates us to continually seek God's answer for the questions and situations we face in our daily lives. Too often, when the answers become too easy, as with the religious leaders of the New Testament, we become heartless in our approach to others and become dependent upon our own answers rather than God.

I was recently reading Second Peter, and a deep sense of dread seemed to come over me. After years in the gospel ministry, I am fearful that many who claim to know Jesus Christ personally may be in for a rude awakening when they face the Master. If I sound a little harsh and condemning, I sincerely and humbly apologize. This is not my goal, but my concern has become even more difficult to ignore almost daily—especially since my retirement and as I have come to realize that through the years I may have unknowingly contributed to this problem. What makes this even more painful is that any attempt to explain my deep-seated concerns are often met with fierce resistance—almost anger—that with my limited abilities, I have found difficult to answer. My fear for the future urges me to warn that continually living in sin is more deadly than any other addiction known to humans, but it hurts deeply to hear their angry words of rejection. My love compels me to fall to me knees and pray to God above that they will see my deep concern through their anger, but it cuts me to the core to see them walk away knowing that our relationship will never be the same. So often their defensiveness is based upon interpretations of the Bible that are different from what I have discovered in the Bible. They are so unlike anything I have been taught through the years by the godly people I admire. From my point of view such positions are so riddled with popular opinion that they stand in stark contrast to what is written in God's Word.

In my perspective, at least in part, this has led to the decline of the church and the turning away from the Lord that we are witnessing among so many of our brothers and sisters in Christ. For years, we have gradually given in to the pressure to make the Word of God more acceptable and less offensive to our congregations, as well as to nonbelievers. This has led us to compromise and to even declare as irrelevant many of the difficult passages found in the Bible. And what have we accomplished? Every day fewer people are coming to know Jesus personally and even fewer are becoming involved in his work, while the demands to compromise the gospel message have become louder. Churches are reaching fewer people than ever, with hundreds of churches closing their doors every year as the individuals who have little, if any, respect for God have become louder and more arrogant in their opposition to traditional biblical teaching. The result of all this is that believers, the church, and the Lord himself have come under ever increasing attacks by the world and the forces of Satan.

Moreover, I believe that this watering down of the gospel has resulted in greater spiritual weakness, and even willful sin among believers. Sadly, many have become so involved in the ways of the world that all resemblance to biblical Christianity has disappeared. For religious leaders to encourage this by compromising the truths of the Bible has served only to place the church and every believer in grave danger. It has led to a reversal of the Lord's teaching on loving God and our neighbor,[3] thus predisposing us to promote love for humans over loving God. It is wrong to proclaim as acceptable all types of immorality and sin based on a distortion of the love taught by the divinely inspired writers. It elevates the imperfect wisdom of sinful humans over the all-knowing, eternal God. In doing so, it places the created above the creator. And even worse, it denies the just and holy nature of God. We simply cannot continue to live to please ourselves without any regard for the divine instructions found in the Bible. We cannot ignore that "All Scripture is given by inspiration of God, and is profitable for doctrine, for reproof, for correction, for instruction in righteousness, that the man of God may be complete, thoroughly equipped for every good work" (2 Timothy 3:16–17 NKJV).

My further question is not how does the world feel about what we are teaching? Rather, how does Jesus Christ feel about this development among those who claim to be his followers?

After much prayer and Bible study, I have come to believe the Lord Jesus Christ feels betrayed once again. I believe he is deeply hurt because individuals who claim his Name have distorted his teaching to support beliefs and actions that are foreign to his holy nature. I find myself fearful that in America today, too many verbalize their love for Jesus, yet they have rejected his eternal love by living in disobedience to his Word. Compromise, self-fulfillment, and tolerance have become the bywords of our day. Each of these have their proper place except when they attempt to supersede the teaching of God. Let's be honest as we consider whether our "righteousness surpasses that of the Pharisees the teachers of the law." Jesus said that unless it does, "You will certainly not enter the kingdom of heaven" (Matthew 5:20 NIV). We must never forget that we are called "to be holy and he is holy ... in conduct and godliness" (1 Peter 1:15–16, 2 Peter 3:11).

This is the reason I have undertaken to write this book—to call God's people back to him. This is the reason I have taken a conservative, and to some, perhaps offensive approach to scripture. *Just Follow Jesus* is an attempt to remind people what the Lord Jesus Christ really meant when he said, "Come follow me." In its most basic sense, this is a call by our Lord to submit ourselves completely unto him. We must call all Christians back to a biblical confession and repentance of our sin, so we might once again become a light in the darkness. We are to endeavor daily to follow our Lord with all our being. If we claim to know Jesus Christ, there is no other optional.

I also believe that all ministers of the gospel are called to follow the example of the apostle Paul as he wrote to the Corinthians:

> We preach Christ crucified: a stumbling block to Jews and foolishness to Gentiles, but to those whom God has called, both Jews and Greeks, Christ the power of God and the wisdom of God. For the foolishness of God is wiser than man's wisdom, and the weakness of God is stronger than man's strength. (1 Corinthians 1:23–25 NIV)

Yes, my stance on the gospel may be offensive to some individuals, but Christianity by its very nature is offensive to those who see it as foolishness. The proclamation of the gospel of Jesus has always been and will continue to be a stumbling block to many who object to the teaching of the Bible. From the beginning of his earthly ministry there have been those individuals and groups who have objected to the Lord's teaching, and hence they have refused to worship and follow the LORD God of heaven and earth. Such will always be the case until the Lord returns and establishes his new kingdom. Some will disagree with what I have written, but if it motives people to consider once again their response to the Master's call, that is all right. After all, try as I might to be accurate, the misinterpretations of scripture and the mistakes in grammar and spelling are all mine, and such things need to be corrected.

With this realization before us, it is my prayer that the reader with an open mind and heart will reconsider his or her relationship with Jesus and make sure he or she is truly following Jesus. Our call from God is to lovingly proclaim the truth of the living gospel to the best of our ability while submitting to the guidance of the Spirit and to let the Holy Spirit convict people and draw them unto God. This may not make any sense to some, but neither does the heavenly Father loving us enough to send his only begotten Son Jesus Christ to die on the cross to redeem us from all our sin.

Praise God that his ways are so different from ours and that his wisdom is greater than our wisdom. God's mercy and grace are beyond our understanding. His love is unlimited and unconditional to all who come to him by faith in his Son Jesus Christ, but lest we forget, someday his patience will come to an end.

May praise be to God the Father and glory to his Son, Jesus the Savior and Lord of heaven and earth. May "the Lamb that was slain receive power and riches and wisdom and might and honor and glory and blessing" (Revelation 5:12 NASB). Amen and amen.

—Billy J. Stines

As he was walking along the Sea of Galilee, he saw two brothers, Simon (who is called Peter), and his brother Andrew. They were casting a net into the sea—for they were fishermen.

"Follow me," he told them, "and I will make you fish for people."

Immediately they left their nets and followed him.

Going on from there, he saw two other brothers, James the son of Zebedee, and his brother John. They were in a boat with Zebedee their father, preparing their nets, and he called them.

Immediately they left the boat and their father and followed him. (Matthew 4:18–22)

Then, as best I can tell, a few days later,

As Jesus went on from there [through the town of Capernaum], he saw a man named Matthew sitting at the toll booth, and he said to him, "Follow me," and he got up and followed him. (Matthew 9:9).

CHAPTER 1

The Call of the Disciples

In a story told by Huston Pastor Tony Evans, an evangelist was invited overseas to minister in a crusade. The first night of his visit, he was picked up by his host and was to be taken to the church where he was to give his message. The car stalled. Upon closer investigation, the driver discovered that his fuel gauge wasn't working, and he had no idea he was out of gas. The driver had, in effect, attempted to take his passengers somewhere with no tiger in his tank! Both the host and the traveling minister had to get out and push the car.

After a while, they were able to get some gas and pour it into the tank. The motor began to rev up because the engine had been fed. Prayer wouldn't have solved that problem. The car even had two holy men in it, but it wouldn't budge without being fed what it required in order to run.

Many of us want to give God everything *except* what God wants. We want to offer God a little of this and a little of that, and then we wonder why our spiritual engines don't roar. God is requiring what we are not giving, and that is a committed life, using the time we have for spiritual development.[4] Diligent scrutiny of the gospel reveals that when we are totally committed to following the Lord, it affects every aspect of our earthly lives from the moment we are saved until we are called home by our Lord and beyond. In Matthew's gospel,[5] we discover insight into this life-changing subject as our Lord calls his first disciples.

Just Ordinary Men

Who were the men called by Jesus? They were two sets of brothers—Peter and Andrew, James and John—and a man whose name was Matthew. From the little we know about them, if we were selecting individuals to follow Jesus, these men would have never been on our list. But Jesus saw something in them we could never see.

In each case, **the men were just working at their daily jobs.** Peter, Andrew, James, and John made their livelihood fishing in the Sea of Galilee. Every day they worked hard to feed their families from what they caught and then most likely sold or traded the rest for whatever else they needed. Luke indicates that they may have just returned from a long, fruitless night of fishing,[6] and they were apparently cleaning and repairing their nets so they could go out again that evening. But Jesus turned their lives upside down by calling to them, saying, "Follow Me."

Likewise, a few days later in the city of Capernaum,[7] Matthew was just going about his daily business. He was at his table (I suspect flanked by a Roman guard) collecting taxes for the hated Roman government from the Jewish people when Jesus walked by and said, "Follow Me."

What jumps out at me from this story is that God often calls ordinary individuals amid their ordinary activities, just as he did with these men. The same has been true throughout history. God called a man named Abram, and as he followed the Lord God by faith, Abram became Abraham and the father of many nations.[8] God placed a young man named Joseph in an Egyptian prison so he could provide a future refuge for his people.[9] He called Moses from the midst of a burning bush while he was tending his father-in-law's sheep just as he had for forty years.[10] Young Samuel was called four separate times while he was sleeping on a mat in the temple before he acknowledged it was God speaking to him.[11] Through Samuel the prophet, the Lord God anointed a teenage named David king of Israel after a long day in the fields tending his family's sheep.[12] The Lord called Elisha to be his prophet through one of his greatest prophets, Elijah, while he was plowing his family's fields.[13] The prophet Isaiah answered God's call while worshipping him in the temple.[14] God called the prophet Amos, a sheepherder, from a relatively obscure town named Tekoa.[15] Mary was appointed the mother of God's son, Jesus, while she was still a teenager.[16] Months after his resurrection, our Lord spoke to Saul from a blinding light as he traveled to Damascus to arrest Christians. Almost immediately, God called Ananias in a vision to restore Saul's sight and rename him Paul because God was sending him to proclaim the gospel unto the Gentiles.[17] Jesus called these men—Peter, James, John, and Andrew, from their fishing nets and Matthew from his tax tables—to follow him.

The simple fact is that Jesus calls people—men and women and boys and girls of all ages, from all walks of life and backgrounds, rich and poor, from all nationalities and races, with different talents and abilities—to a life of service. I was called by our heavenly Father just a few months before my sixteenth birth, first to salvation, and then, a few months later, to the gospel ministry. After the call to salvation, the call to service is the most important call every believer must answer. Every believer is called to serve Jesus wherever he has placed us in life.

In addition, **each of the men made the choice to follow Jesus—** and notice, it was an immediate choice. The opening chapter of John's gospel tells us that they had already meet Jesus; therefore, they already knew something about him. Andrew had spent the afternoon in his presence, and then he had brought Peter to the Messiah.[18] As they listened to his teaching, his amazing words of life

3

had already gained a foothold in their imaginations. It also seems likely they had witnessed more than a few miracles as Jesus began his public ministry. That further fostered a sense of wonderment about him. When Jesus said, "Follow Me," these four fishermen did not need to think about whether to follow him. They did not stop to debate whether it was wise to follow him. They did not need anyone's permission or to check a public opinion poll. They did not even stop to consider how following Jesus might affect their families or friends. Instead, they just left their fishing boats and nets and followed Jesus.

Likewise, while sitting in his tax booth in Capernaum along the busy caravan route between Damascus to the northeast and the Mediterranean Sea to the west,[19] Matthew had most likely heard of Jesus. Because he was collecting taxes for the hated Roman government, he was considered a traitor by the Jewish people. Many thought him to be as vile as any thief because his wages were whatever he collected above the required taxes. But Jesus saw something different, and when he called, Matthew immediately followed.

This same decision is ours. When the Lord God calls, we have a choice to make—whether to follow him. If we pause long enough to debate all the issues involved in that call, more than likely, we will come up with some reason not to respond. Fear may invade our thoughts and lead us to reject his call. The same is true regardless of whether we are talking about coming to salvation or surrendering to some form of ministry. In some mysterious miracle of grace, by his Spirit, God draws us to himself,[20] and we respond to his loving call. At the same time, we decide to come believing in him and surrendering to Lordship, we also choose to be his representatives in whatever walk of life we find ourselves.

Did you catch what I just said?

An interesting fact about following Jesus is that the gospels indicate that by answering the call of Jesus to salvation, we are also answering the call to become his personal servants. In scripture, the two are so linked together that they cannot be separated. Regardless of what we may believe, one does not occur without the other, even though it is easier to speak of them as two separate events.

This brings us to a troubling thought about following Jesus. The Bible makes it clear that if we are unwilling to be his representatives before others, we have not committed ourselves to him.[21] Jesus said, "He who is not with me is against me" (Matthew 12:30). If we have not surrendered utterly to him, we may not be his followers, regardless of what we may claim. I did not say this—Jesus did, more than once and in several ways. It is the same for the individual of whom Jesus speaks in the parable of the sower.[22] Explaining the parable to his disciples, Jesus said, "The one who received the seed that fell on rocky places is the man who hears the word and at once receives it with joy. But since he has no root, he lasts only a short time. When trouble or persecution comes because of the word, he quickly falls away (Matthew 13:20–21 NIV).

So often we ignore this point. The man of whom Jesus spoke in this parable had made only a "temporary" (NASB) commitment unto Jesus. The New King James Version says he "endures only for a while." His faith in the Lord had "no root," and as soon as he encountered "distress or persecution … he falls away." In other words, when things change for the worse, he "falls away" to no longer follow Jesus.

The phrase "no root" brings forth two ideas. The first concerns a house that was built upon a foundation of sand, and when the rains and wind came, it fails and is destroyed by the storm.[23] This implies that the human who "falls away" does not truly believe in Christ; thus when troubles come, he or she is driven away. He had only made a temporary commitment to Jesus, he abandons him due to distress or persecution. The second idea regarding "no root" focuses on the root of a plant, which penetrates the soil and draws up the nourishment and water needed for the plant to grow. Here the logical implication is that the one who "falls away" has not received the spiritual nourishment necessary to grow in the Lord.

Just as a plant dies without nourishment, so does a person without spiritual nourishment. In either case, the man who hears the word later "falls away" because he has "no root." He is like the blueberry bush I planted one spring. He had "no root" and when the heat of the summer began to bear down on him, he dried up and died.

On the night of his arrest, Jesus warned of such a possibility as he said, "All this I have told you so that you will not fall away" (John 16:1 NIV). The Beloved Apostle John described such individuals this way:

> They went out from us, but they did not belong to us; for if they had belonged to us, they would have remained with us. However, they went out so that it might be made clear that none of them belongs to us. (1 John 2:19)

The sad truth is that not everyone who claims to know Jesus is a follower of Jesus. For whatever reason—whether it is affliction, persecution, prosperity, or involvement in sin—some will "fall away" from him. They will desert Jesus and return to the ways of the world. Every pastor has witnessed that individual who apparently came to Christ and for a time appeared to be very faithful, but at some point, he or she simply disappears. One day we suddenly miss that person, only to discover he or she is off living in and for the world once again. As church leaders, we are left wondering what happened. Was the profession of faith real or was he or she merely caught up in the moment? The simple truth is, Jesus will say to some who claim to know him, "I never knew you" (Matthew 7:23).

On the other hand, the scriptures also states that all who are saved will receive "the Spirit of adoption" as sons of God (Romans 8:15) and are called to a life of serving Christ. At first, we may not understand the exact nature of our service to Jesus. Neither can we see what the future may hold after we answer the Lord's call. Furthermore, there is the real possibility that we may receive an additional call into a different form of service further down life's road, but we are called to serve him from the moment of our salvation. We are called to be his ambassadors, his witnesses, his servants. At the very least, we are called to tell the lost about Jesus and what he has done in our lives.

This call to service is evident in the response of different individuals who meet Jesus during his earthly ministry. For instance, the woman Jesus met at the well went into town and declared, "Come, see a man who told me all things that I have done; this is not the Christ, is it?" and the people came to believe in Jesus (John 4:29, 39 NASB). She met Jesus and he changed her life so much that she had to tell someone about it. On another occasion, after healing two blind men, Jesus instructed them, "Don't tell anyone about this." But we are told that when Jesus and his disciples had departed, "they went out and spread his fame all over the region" (Matthew 9:27–31 NLT). We find much the same at the extremes of his time on earth. At his birth, after seeing "Mary and Joseph … and the babe, lying in a manger," the shepherds shared with everyone they met all the things that they had seen and heard (Luke 2:16, 18, 20 NLT). Likewise, after meeting the resurrected Lord in the garden an excited Mary Magdalene came running from the empty tomb shouting to the disciples, 'I've seen the Lord. He is alive' (John 20:18).

It is the same with us, especially in the days following our conversion. As new believers in Christ, we are more likely to tell other people about Jesus. When we meet Jesus in a life-changing way, we must tell someone. It is true about any life-changing event in our lives, and it is true about meeting Jesus. We just can't keep it in; nor should we keep it to ourselves. We've got to tell someone the good news. As servants of the living Lord, we are compelled to tell others with the same compassion Jesus showed for the physically sick.

When God calls us personally, a transformation begins to take place in our lives that will affect every area of our life. We are new creatures in Christ.[24] As we present ourselves to God as instruments of righteousness,[25] we are used by him to proclaim his message of redemption and forgiveness to those in need of salvation. As we yield ourselves into him, the indwelling Spirit leads us into an even more personal relationship with Christ Jesus as "heirs of God and coheirs with Christ" (Romans 8:16–17).

Notice further, **these men left everything to follow Jesus**. Peter, Andrew, James and John were fishermen, so when Jesus said, "Follow Me," they left their boats and their nets. They left their fathers with the other laborers. Nowhere are we told they had their father's approval. They just left. Apparently from this moment, as they followed Jesus, they spent very little time with their families, although it appears Peter may have turned his home in Capernaum into a base of operations during their Galilean ministry.[26] [27] They left their livelihood to follow Jesus, perhaps as some have suggested, returning once in a while to earn a living for their families.[28] But outwardly it appears that without thought, they dissolved their fishing partnership and Peter Andrew, James and John followed Jesus. In Luke's accord, we are told they "left everything and followed him" (Luke 5:10–11).

Likewise, Matthew left everything to follow Jesus. The gospel accounts tell us that he got up and immediately followed Jesus. In other words, he left his tax collection business and all his wealth to follow Jesus. It seems he left behind his equally despised friends because we hear very little about them after the supper he threw to introduce Jesus to them.[29] This also means he left his employment as tax collector for the Roman Empire, as well as the social status that came with it—just to follow Jesus. But unlike the fishermen who could return to their nets and did for a short time after the resurrection,[30] Matthew could not go back to his job of being a tax collector. It had already been granted to another individual; therefore, among the disciples, Matthew no doubt made the greatest material sacrifice of his possessions. But he was willing to pay the cost[31] because according to Luke, he also left "everything behind … and began to follow him" (Luke 5:38).

A third spiritual truth comes to mind. When we follow Jesus, we surrender completely to his calling. Just as a conquered army will surrender unconditionally to the victor, we are to surrender unconditionally to Jesus. By his death on the cross, Jesus has won the victory over temptation and sin. Now he stands ready to forgive us completely and supply our every need. By defeating the power of sin and death, Jesus offers us a new life in him, but we must come unconditionally to him by faith and surrender our lives to him. There can be no straddling the fence of commitment. We cannot serve God and mammon.[32] We cannot continue to live a life of sin and follow Jesus at the same time. The Beloved Disciple stated this clearly.

> Everyone who remains in him does not sin; everyone who sins has not seen him or known him. … Everyone who has been born of God does not sin … This is how God's children and the devil's children become obvious. Whoever does not do what is right is not of God, especially the one who does not love his brother or sister. (1 John 3:9–10)

We are not called to make a half-hearted commitment unto Jesus. We must leave everything and give Jesus complete control of our lives and follow him!

Robert Chapman of Bamstaple, a great friend of the late George Muller of Bristol, was once asked, "Would you not advise young Christians to do something for the Lord?"

"No," was the reply. "I should advise them to do everything for the Lord."[33] Paul also challenged us toward this goal.

> Whatever you do, in word or in deed, do everything in the name of the Lord Jesus … Whatever you do,

> work heartily, as for the Lord and not for men … You
> serve the Lord Christ. (Colossians 3:17–24 ESV)

My friend, are you serving Jesus in your everyday life? What is it like to follow Jesus? For the first disciples, what did they expect when they left everything to follow him? Did these early disciples even know what would be demanded of them?

They Were Ordinary Men with an Extraordinary Mission

As we consider these questions, we need to understand something that is very important, which we often overlook. **These men followed Jesus to become fishers of men.** Most of us can recall Matthew's or Mark's account of Jesus's call of these first disciples, but Luke tells a different side of the story in the fifth chapter of his gospel.[34] It seems that during the day, Jesus used Peter and Andrew's boat as a platform to teach the multitude that had follow him seeking a miracle. At the conclusion of his instruction, Jesus told them to push out into the Sea of Galilee and lower their fishing nets. At first Peter voiced the objected that they were tired after a long fruitless night, but because Jesus said, "Let's go fishing," he deferred to Jesus. His obedience was rewarded with so many fish that their nets began to break. Calling for help from their partners James and John, they brought in the catch, which was so enormous that it filled both boats. Once they arrived back at the shore, in amazement Peter fell to his knees before Jesus and exclaimed, "Go away from me because I'm a sinful man, Lord" (v. 8). To which Jesus replied:

> "Do not be afraid. … From now on you will be catching men." … then they … left everything and followed Him. (Luke 5:10–11)

Similar words are also recorded in Matthew's and Mark's accounts.[35] So what did Jesus mean—"from now on you will be catching men"? Although they were fishermen, at that moment, did Peter, Andrew, James, and John even understand what Jesus meant? Likewise, did Matthew comprehend what he was getting into as he left his tax job to follow Jesus?

Probably not, especially since on several occasions Jesus reprimanded them for their little faith.[36] But each of them learned over the next three years as they followed him from place to place listening to his teaching, witnessing his miracles and seeing lives changed. When they were sent by Jesus in pairs to declare his message and heal the nation of Israel, for a time they experienced a glimpse of what Jesus meant.[37] Later, after they were almost crushed by his death on the cross, their hearts and minds were uplifted as Jesus enlightened them regarding the truth of the law and prophets during the days after our Lord's resurrection. They came to a more complete understanding of what he meant on the day of Pentecost as the Holy Spirit came upon them, and they proclaimed the message of Jesus Christ with such power that three thousand souls were saved.[38] They were to tell people about Jesus, and they did so no matter the opposition that beset them everywhere they went.

What we see here is too powerful to ignore. Jesus said, "'I will make you fishers of men.'" As the disciples followed him, Jesus trained and prepared them by example and through his teaching. He also gave them practical training as he sent them out in twos on two separate occasions to proclaim the kingdom of God, to heal the sick, and to cast out demons.[39] Then, by his Spirit, he empowered them to carry on his mission of declaring the kingdom of God as he returned to the Father. We have the same empowerment from on high as we seek to fulfill the same task the Lord gave his first disciples—to be fisher of men. We are to prepare ourselves by every means possible to go forth and catch men, women, boys, and girls—old and young alike—for Jesus. By the Spirit, we proclaim the gospel of Jesus Christ whenever possible, wherever possible, by any means available to us. The Great Commission given by our Lord makes this very clear.

> Go therefore and make disciples of all the nations, baptizing them in the name of the Father and of the Son and of the Holy Spirit, teaching them to observe all things that I have commanded you; and lo, I am with you always, even to the end of the age. Amen! (Matthew 28:19–20 NKJV)

> Go into all the world and preach the gospel to every creature. (Mark 16:15 NKJV)

> You shall receive power when the Holy Spirit has come upon you; and you shall be witnesses to me in Jerusalem, and in all Judea and Samaria, and to the end of the earth. (Acts 1:8 NKJV)

Just as in the days following Pentecost, we are to proclaim Jesus, and the Lord will give the increase.[40] During the course of living our daily lives, we are to tell others about Jesus and what he accomplished through his death on the cross and his resurrection from the tomb. By our words, actions, and reactions, we are to teach them what it means to have a personal relationship with Jesus. We are to baptize them, teach them, and show them how they are to go about their daily lives, so that they too might proclaim Jesus—teach and show other people how to have a personal relationship with Jesus—so they might also go forth and do the same to even more people. In terms often heard today among pastors, we are to produce disciples who go forth to share the gospel of Jesus Christ and service others in brotherly love—not just make church members. Jesus said a few hours before his arrest in the garden: "You did not choose Me, but I chose you, and I appointed you to go and bear fruit and that your fruit should remain" (John 15:16 NASB).

Announcing the call to be a follower of Jesus involves living every day, every moment in a personal relationship with him. It involves giving one's self completely to his teaching and showing people how to live for our Lord through both our words and actions. It is loving others as Jesus loves us. It is giving feet and voice to our best intentions of telling people about Jesus.

In his defense before Agrippa and Festus, Paul said, "I preached that they should repent and turn to God and demonstrate their repentance by their deeds" (Acts 26:20 NIV). This should also be our goal as we seek to follow Jesus.

Summarizing the Lord's call to "follow Me," one commentator wrote: "Packed into this two-word command are many implications. Jesus was saying, 'Live with me and learn by watching me. Own my values and priorities. Learn to become passionate for the things I live for. And follow my example by doing the ministry I have come to do.'"[41]

The story is told of a small boy who closely watched a neighboring pastor build a wooden trellis to support a climbing vine. The youngster did not say a word the entire time that he watched. Pleased at the thought that his work was being admired, the pastor finally said to the boy, "Well, son, trying to pick up some pointers on gardening?"

"No," replied the boy, "I'm just waiting to hear what a preacher says when he hits his thumb with a hammer."[42]

We need to also understand that as we seek to bring people to the Savior, **our lives should be living proof that we follow Jesus.** To do otherwise is to accomplish the opposite of our goal of being fishers of men. Throughout his ministry, the apostle Paul had always sought to declare Jesus Christ as the One who reconciled us unto God. Looking back at his life, his concern was that he "put no stumbling block in anyone's path" (2 Corinthians 6:3 NIV). Simply stated, Paul did not want to be the reason someone did not come to know Jesus Christ; therefore, in response, he wrote, "As God's ministers, we commend ourselves in everything" (2 Corinthians 6:4).

The meaning of "in everything" should be clear to each of us. It includes everything we are and hope to be, everything we own, everything we think about, everything we do or say, every reaction and response, every situation of life—whether a difficulty or an opportunity to rejoice—should "commend us as servants of God" (NASB). But what does the word *commend* mean?

In the Greek (συνστημι) *commend* means "to certify or to recommend a stranger."[43] The idea is of introducing ourselves with the connotation of proving ourselves.[44] So Paul is essentially saying, "We do not need anyone or any letter of introduction from a second party to introduce us and tell you who we are. You have already seen the proof and know that we are 'God's ministers.'" Then, in the verses that following, Paul offered a long list of twenty-eight living proofs that he was a servant of God.

> As God's ministers, we commend ourselves in everything: by great endurance, by afflictions, by hardships, by difficulties, by beatings, by imprisonments, by riots, by labors, by sleepless nights, by times of hunger, by purity, by knowledge, by patience, by kindness, by the Holy Spirit, by sincere love, by the word of truth, by the power of God; through the weapons of righteousness for the right hand and the left, through glory and dishonor, through slander and good redeemer; regarded as deceivers, yet true; as unknown, yet recognized; as dying, yet see—we live; as disciplined, yet not killed, as grieving, yet always rejoicing; as poor yet enriching many; as having nothing, yet possessing everything. (2 Corinthians 6:4–10)

Plainly stated, the way Paul lived his life in the midst of everything that came his way —both the good and bad things—was all the proof that was needed for the Corinthians to know that he was a servant of God. His life was the only validation that was needed to testify that he was a follower of Jesus Christ. Apparently, the same could be said of Peter and John as the Jewish High Court saw their "boldness ... perceived that they were uneducated and untrained men ... and ... recognized that they had been with Jesus." Or of believers in Antioch as "the disciples were first called Christians" (Acts 4:13; 11:26 NKJV). The same should be said of anyone who claims to personally know Jesus as Lord and Savior. When we follow Jesus, we do not need people to say, "He is a believer in Jesus," or "She lived as a Christian." This should be self-evident to everyone as we endure both the good and bad that life throws our way. How we live our lives should be all that is necessary to prove our total surrender unto Jesus Christ as Lord of our lives.

In the Sermon on the Mount, our Lord stated it very plainly: "You will know them by their fruits" (Matthew 7:16, 20 NKJV). Seeing the godly fruit of our lives, the people around us should know we have a daily personal relationship with him. The individuals we work with will recognize the character of Jesus Christ shining forth through our day-by-day action and reactions. The persons we live with will hear his voice in what we say and how we say it. Even the people we meet casually during our daily lives will recognize there is something different about us.

Jesus said the same things to his disciples in the upper room.

> A new command I give you: Love one another. As I have loved you, so you must love one another. By this all men will know that you are my disciples, if you love one another. (John 13:34–35 NIV)

How we express our love for one another is living proof that we are his disciples. The way we live should help people know without a shadow of doubt that we have been with Jesus.

Every day I pause and ask myself, *Can this be said of me?* Can it be said of you?

In my reading, I came across a rather humorous but revealing

story. A man one day was writing the love of his life—her name was
Betty. He wrote:

> My dearest Betty,
>
> I love you beyond words. Webster does not have in
> his dictionary the necessary vocabulary to explain
> the depth of my love for you. Thoughts of you
> dance across the portals of my mind. You are my all-
> consuming passion. So enraptured am I regarding
> my love for you that the Pacific Ocean would be
> like a pond if I had to swim it. I could do it as long
> as I knew you were awaiting me on the other shore.
> The heat of the Sahara Desert would never impede
> my progress to you, knowing that you would be the
> oasis that would refresh me when I arrive. There
> would be no inconvenience I wouldn't endure for
> you. Climbing Mount Everest would only seem like
> getting over an ant's hill if I knew you were at the
> precipice. All I'm simply saying to you, my darling,
> is that my love for you transcends time and space.
>
> Signed, Sam.
> PS: I'll see you Saturday night if it doesn't rain.

Now I'm sure you would agree that Sam was only full of a bunch
of noise. Sam could talk a good game, but he didn't go very deep.
While he could verbalize overcoming the elements to get to his love,
a little bit of rain would keep him away.[45]

My friends, it is easy to verbalize our love for our Lord and our
commitment to follow him when life is easy. But it is an entirely
different matter to surrender one's life completely to Jesus and strive
daily to follow him through the bad times, as well as the good times;
through the happy moments of life and the hours of distress, sorry,

and pain; through the times of persecution and tribulation; through personal sacrifice and service. If we are to completely follow Jesus, we must also ask ourselves: Do we just talk a good game, or do we truly follow Jesus with all our being?

A hymn written by B. B. McKinney nearly a century ago captured the essence of what it means to follow Jesus.

> While passing through this world of sin,
> And to others your life shall view,
> Be clean and pure without, within,
> Let others see Jesus in you.
>
> Let others see Jesus in you,
> Let others see Jesus in you;
> Keep telling the story, be faithful and true,
> Let others see Jesus in you.[46]

Food for Thought

Do you have a personal relationship with Jesus Christ?

How would you describe your call to a personal relationship with Jesus?

In your daily life, are you a "fisher of men"?

Where do you see the Lord leading you in the future?

Do other people see Jesus in your life?

If anyone wants to follow after me, let him deny himself, take up his cross daily, and follow me.

For whoever wants to save his life will lose it, but whoever loses his life because of me will save it.

For what does it benefit someone if he gains the whole world, and yet loses or forfeits himself?

For whoever is ashamed of me and my words, the Son of Man will be ashamed of him when he comes in his glory and that of the Father and the holy angels.

Truly I tell you, there are some standing here who will not taste death until they see the kingdom of God. (Luke 9:23–27)

CHAPTER 2

The Call to the Cross

While I serving on the staff of my first church, in Jackson, South Carolina, I had the privilege of being among the first in the area to study *MasterLife* as developed by Avery Willis. It was an unbelievable study in discipleship, particularly for a young minister fresh out of the seminary, and it greatly influenced my life. In fact, down through the years I have frequently stopped to meditate on many of the scripture passages we were encouraged to study and to memorize and make a part of our lives. One such challenging passage comes from the ninth chapter of the Gospel of Luke. To the one who claims to be a disciple of Jesus, these words are some of the most challenging and yet disturbing ever spoken by the Master.

The Disciple's Cross

To this point in his earthly ministry, there had been only veiled allusions to our Lord's coming crucifixion and resurrection, which were often misunderstood or completely ignored. John the Baptist presented him to his own followers as the "Lamb of God" (John 1:29). A few weeks later, as he cleansed the temple, Jesus referred to the destruction of the temple as he anticipated his own death.[47]

In his conversation with Nicodemus, Jesus compared himself to the serpent that was raised up in the wilderness.[48] He later made reference to the three days Jonah spent in the belly of the whale as a sign of his death and resurrection.[49] But from this moment, his predictions became clearer as he prepared the disciples for his future suffering on the cross.

Like Matthew,[50] Luke recorded these words on the heels of Peter's confession that Jesus was "the Christ of God" (Luke 9:20). By openly talking of his death and resurrection, Jesus left little doubt that he was referring to his death on the cross. Instead of making it easy to follow him, the Good Shepherd challenged his followers to literally "come after" him—all the way to the cross and beyond.

To begin with, **a disciple of Jesus has a "desire" to follow him**. Jesus began by saying, "If anyone wants to follow after me ..."

Do you remember the Lays potato chip slogan from a few years ago? "You can't eat just one." Many of us have tried, only to acknowledge our failure as we crumbled up the empty bag to throw it in the trash. Such a craving happens because the ingredients of the potato chip produced an almost undeniable desire within the taste buds on our tongues that we felt we *needed* another potato chip.

When we yearn for Jesus, something similar happens to us spiritually. The Bible says, "Like newborn babies, crave pure spiritual milk, so that by it you may grow up in your salvation" (1 Peter 2:2 NIV). When my young grandchildren need to eat, they make themselves very clear. There can be no delay; they want to eat now! The same desire must be ours. As we come to Jesus and surrender ourselves unto the indwelling power of the Spirit, a desire to experience the fulness of Jesus Christ begins to develop in our lives. We are drawn closer and closer to him. As we listen to the small still voice of the Holy Spirit, an inward yearning to know more about Jesus takes root within us. When we feed that desire with the spiritual food of Bible study, prayer, and godly service, it continues to grow and mature. There wells up within us a deep thirst to experience more of the living water of Jesus Christ.[51] We find ourselves craving more of the bread of life, which is Christ Jesus our Lord.[52]

Throughout his life, David developed such a longing. As a result, he began the forty-second Psalm saying, "As the deer pants for the water brooks, So pants my soul for You, O God. My soul thirsts for God, for the living God" (Psalm 42:1–2 NKJV). As we study his imperfect life, it quickly becomes evident that he was a man after God's own heart. We see through the Psalms that the more David focused on God, the more he wanted to know and experience God's presence. Ideally, this is the same attitude that every follower of Jesus Christ should exhibit. There should be a deep-seated ache within our soul to know our Savior more and more. And when sin separates us from him, like King David, we come crawling back to him pleading for his forgiveness and restoration.[53]

We see this same desire in the lives of his disciples. As Jesus walked on the earth, there was something about him that drew people to him and produced a longing within them to be in his presence. But the day after feeding the five thousand, many became disenchanted and began to desert him as his teaching became more difficult to understand and accept. Turning to the twelve, Jesus asked, "You don't want to go away too, do you?" Seemingly without hesitation, Peter declared, "Lord, to whom shall we go? You have the words of eternal life." Then he made a statement of faith in Jesus that we often miss—"We believe and know that you are the Messiah, the only Son of God" (John 6:68–69).

Please remember the circumstances. Some among the crowd had left him because he refused to perform a miracle and feed them again. Others simply overwhelmed by his demanding teaching began to wander away. Meanwhile, in anger and jealousy the religious leaders reacted by secretly discussing ways to kill him due to his claims.[54] And yet, somehow it appears that the light of his life-giving words was beginning to penetrate through the crack Jesus had opened into the disciples' lives. So much so that when Jesus said in the last weeks of his ministry, "Our friend Lazarus ... is died ... But let's go to him," Thomas was able to say, "Let's go too so that we may die with him" (John 11:11–16). Did they understand everything about the implications of his possible death? Obviously not, but the divine spark was there. I imagine it would have been more difficult to have made such a statement a year or so earlier. But during the months between the two events, as they followed Jesus, the Holy Spirit worked to draw them even closer to him, but they still had a way to go. The events surrounding his crucifixion revealed just how small their faith truly was, but God's divine presence was producing a longing to know Jesus more. God the Father was slowly drawing the disciples to his Only Begotten Son Jesus Christ.

Sadly, instead of seeking Jesus, too many people attempt to fulfill their own desires in other ways. Just think about it for a moment. In today's society we are out for "me, myself, and I." At heart, we are a selfish people who want above all else to satisfy our own personal desires. When we do good things for other people, it is often to make us feel good about ourselves and to be praised by others. This has been our nature since our childhood. The Bible says, "All have sinned and come short of the glory of God" (Romans 3:23 KJV). Scripture declares that without Christ we are slaves to our sinful natures.[55] This is most evident in our endless search for more possessions, for more popularity, for a more prestigious and powerful position, and as we seek more money to help us achieve these goals. In our old sinful nature, we are continually looking for happiness as defined by the society. "Enticed by fleshly desires" (2 Peter 2:18–19 NASB), we are constantly trying to satisfy our sinful lust, while seldom finding lasting contentment.

No one is exempt from such a temptation because we live in a sinful world. Every believer battles temptation and sin throughout his or her life, even the apostle Paul. In Romans, he described his own personal fight and concluded that the source of his struggles was the "sin living in me" (Romans 7:17, 20). But when we give ourselves to Jesus, the Spirit helps us in the fight. We find strength to overcome sin and temptation through his indwelling presence. There develops within our soul a deep-seated ache to better know our Savior. Having this same longing, Paul wrote in his letter to the Philippians: "My goal is to know him and the power of his resurrection and the fellowship of his sufferings, being conformed to his death, assuming that I will somehow reach the resurrection from among the dead" (Philippians 3:10–11). But understand this: The daily battle with temptation and sin is very real. Just as Jesus faced temptation from Satan in the wilderness and overcame it,[56] so can we, if we remain focused on the Lord Jesus Christ. And when we yield to temptation, and because of our human nature there is an excellent chance we will, God is ready to forget our sin and cleanse us from all unrighteousness.[57]

Beginning with words from the pen of David, another songwriter caught the deep desire we should have for God with these words.

> As the deer panteth for the water,
> so my soul longeth after Thee,
> You alone are my heart's desire
> and I long to worship Thee.
> You alone are my strength my shield.
> To You alone may my spirit yield.
> You alone are my heart's desire
> and I long to worship Thee.[58]

Also, coming from his desire to know him, **a disciple of Jesus will "deny himself."** Here the Lord is calling on the believer to once and for all say no to his old self. We are to give up any reliance upon self and our own abilities and place our dependence for salvation on God alone. Moreover, we acknowledge our utter inability to please God on our own. In humble confession, we seek to turn away from all thoughts and habits that indicate an attitude of self-reliance and pride and fall spiritually broken before the throne of God. The simple truth is that when we deny ourselves, "self" is no longer in charge of our lives—God is. In turn, we exhibit a new willingness to say with the apostle Paul: "Everything that was a gain to me, I have considered to be a loss because of Christ" (Philippians 3:7).

How does this change happen? It is a transformation that occurs as we deny our own sinful desires and delight ourselves in the Lord. Gradually we deliberately turn our focus from pleasing self to pleasing our Lord. As we intentionally seek the Father who is reaching out to us, our lives are transformed by the power of the Holy Spirit, and we discover that our wants have changed. We learn to want what God desires for us. Slowly, through the power of the Spirit, as we purposely spend time with God, what was once important to us becomes less essential to our happiness. As we follow Christ, the things of the world become less critical to us, and a zeal for the things of God begins to take root in our hearts and lives. As we focus upon the Lord, his delights and his desires become our delights and our desires, and a godly contentment begins to grow in our lives. As we surrender to the influence of the Holy Spirit upon our lives, we are changed from the inside out, and a greater longing to know Jesus grows within us. By focusing on the LORD God, we develop a desire to please God rather than ourselves, and by his Holy Spirit he blesses us with a contentment in life from on high.

The apostle Paul expressed his growing contentment this way in his letter to the Philippians: "I rejoiced greatly in the Lord … for I have learned to be content in whatever circumstances" (Philippians 4:10–11 NIV). First, notice Paul "learned to be content." It was not something that came naturally to him. Yes, this would imply that Paul had weak moments when the never-ending earthly battles against temptation seemed almost lost. But through personal trial and error, success and failure, and a daily dependence upon the living God, he learned through it all to be content by being in the presence of his Lord Jesus Christ. In his letter to the Corinthians, Paul showed us just how content he had become as he wrote, "I am well content with weaknesses, with insults, with distresses, with persecutions, with difficulties, for Christ's sake; when I am weak, then I am strong" (2 Corinthians 12:10 NASB).

Can you imagine? Through a life of hardship and adversity, Paul had learned to be content in the middle of the most difficult of circumstances because his chief concern was "for Christ's sake." Can any one of us say this? *God's Word Translation* expresses where Paul was in his own personal journey with God this way: "Christ means everything to me in this life" (Philippians 1:21 GW).

Can you imagine being able to truthfully say this about your life: "Christ means everything to me in this life"? In all honesty, I find myself a little uneasy just thinking about this level of commitment because I know I'm not there yet. I still have a long way to go in achieving such commitment. There are still things and individuals in my life that mean more to me than the Lord. What about you? Does it make you uneasy as well? Are there individuals and things that mean more to you than Jesus Christ? The truth is, as we deny self by the power of the Holy Spirit, we literally make Christ everything in our lives.

Moreover, **a disciple of Jesus will "take up his cross."** This simple phrase calls to mind the picture of a condemned man who under duress has been forced to take the crossbars of his cross upon his shoulders and carry it to the place of his execution. Lest we forget, in the Roman world the cross was an instrument of execution. It symbolized the shame, guilt, suffering, and rejection of the individual who was destined to hang suspended between heaven and earth by nails driven in his hands and feet. There was no more despicable way to die. But also realize this: what the convicted would do under duress, the disciple of Jesus Christ does freely and willingly. Taking up one's cross is the ultimate denial of self. In love and loyalty, the disciple of Jesus Christ voluntarily accepts all the pain, all the shame, and all the suffering of the cross for the cause of Christ.[59]

There can be little doubt that "those who follow Jesus can expect to be ridiculed and to be frequently persecuted, and perhaps even killed."[60] There are numerous occasions in the book of Acts when this happened. From the beginning of the church, we discover Peter and John being beaten and imprisoned by the religious leaders.[61] Stephen was martyred,[62] followed sometime later by the beheading of James.[63] Persecution forced Christians in Jerusalem to scatter throughout the Roman Empire.[64] In much of the remaining accounts of the early church, we are confronted by the sufferings endured by the apostle Paul and his associates as they sought to spread the gospel throughout the Roman Empire. One such event finds Paul and Silas beaten and bleeding in the dungeon of a Philippian prison, and yet, by faith they were able to praise God with praying and singing.[65] Summing up his life, the apostle Paul wrote the Corinthians, "I die daily" (1 Corinthians 15:17 NKJV).

Noted Bible scholar and teacher Warren Wiersbe offers us this additional insight.

> We must first say no to ourselves—not simply to pleasures or possessions, but to self—and then take up our cross and follow Christ daily. This means to be identified with him in surrender, suffering, and sacrifice. You cannot crucify yourself; you can only yield your body (Romans 12:1–2) and let God do the rest.[66]

With this challenge, Jesus insisted that the one who follows him must freely "take up his cross" with a willingness to suffer anything, even persecution and death, for him. In the days that followed, as the persecution of Christians grew throughout the Roman Empire, these words by the Savior encouraged the embattled believers to hold on to their faith and endure the injustice and hatred they faced on earth, while focusing on the coming kingdom of God.

Down through the ages, there are many examples of such selfless sacrifice for the cause of Christ. The biography *The Shadow of the*

Almighty records this beautiful prayer of sacrifice and surrender uttered by Jim Elliot:

> Father, take my life, yea, my blood if Thou wilt, and consume it with Thine enveloping fire. I would not save it, for it is not mine to save. Have it, Lord, have it all. Pour out my life as an oblation for the world. Blood is only of value as it flows before Thine altar.

Young Jim Elliot went on to willingly shoulder his cross in missionary service, literally sealing it with his own blood at the hands of primitive spearmen deep in the jungles of Ecuador.[67]

Furthermore, **a disciple will follow Jesus "daily."** The emphasis here is on faithfulness. Being a disciple of Jesus Christ requires that we be steadfast in our daily walk with him. Regardless of what we may assert, those who skip church often seeking pleasure in shopping, sporting events, or other activities are not "daily" in their Christian experience. Their actions show a lack of commitment, and, therefore, they will not make a good disciple of Jesus Christ.

Most of us have gone on vacation. A number of years ago, Susan and I vacationed for a few days in the Bahamas. Several days before we left, as I was talking with the church treasurer, he said something that has troubled me ever since that day. He said, "While you're away, let your hair down. If you want to take a drink or even get a little drunk, who cares? No one will ever know." Yes, the chances were that no one would ever know what I had done on my vacation. But I would know. Susan would know. And what is more important, God would know. Besides, there is always the chance that my actions could keep someone I met on my vacation from Jesus Christ. Naturally the opportunity came for us to "let our hair down" on a snorkeling trip in which nearly everyone overindulged on alcohol. But it also became a chance to share how we were having a good time drinking fruit punch instead of an alcoholic beverage.

I beg you, please understand this: we can take a vacation from our jobs and other things in life, but let me be perfectly clear—if Jesus is our Lord, we are never truly on vacation. No matter how far you may travel from home, you are always on duty for Jesus. We cannot let our hair down for an instant because sin may creep into our lives, leading us from Jesus, as well as damaging our witness and preventing someone from coming to Jesus. You see, following Jesus is a daily discipline. It is a full-time job, not a weekend hobby. "Be alert and of sober mind. Your enemy the devil prowls around like a roaring lion, looking for anyone he can devour" and destroy (1 Peter 5:8 NIV). To overcome him, we must seek to follow Jesus day after day, one step at a time.

In his first letter, Peter wrote:

> Just as he who called you is holy, so be holy in all you do … For you know … that you were redeemed … with the precious blood of Christ, a lamb without blemish or defect. (1 Peter 1:15, 18–19 NIV)

My friends, because we "were redeemed … with the precious blood of Christ," we are to always conduct ourselves in a way that brings nothing but honor to the Lord Jesus Christ. To do otherwise is to bring disgrace upon his holy name.

This suggests that **a disciple will keep on following Jesus**. Jesus plainly said, "and follow me." Commentators tell us that the Greek implies that once a person begins to follow, the disciple of Jesus Christ must keep on following Jesus. There is not turning aside for personal reasons. There can be no going back and taking a different track in life. There is no mulligan in our Christian life. We are to be obedient to our Lord in every area of our lives because our obedience is the scale by which our love for him is measured. Several times in different ways in the upper room Jesus said, "If you love me, you will keep my commandments."[68] We are to be so devoted to him that nothing draws us away from him. The fundamental idea here is that the Master calls us to keep on trusting him,[69] to keep on walking in his footsteps[70] and to keep on obeying his commands.[71] And we do so out of a heartfelt gratitude for the salvation he has so graciously offered unto us out of his boundless love.[72]

Sound impossible doesn't it? It is—for you and me in our own strength. We need the moment-by-moment presence of the Holy Spirit working in our lives, and even then, at times we will falter and give in to temptation and sin. But always remember God has promised to forgive us and restore our broken relationship with him. This is not a license to live as we please without any regard for God's holy word; rather, it is a reminder that God loves us so much that he always stands ready to renew our relationship when it is broken by sin.

The Disciple's Devotion

Have you ever lost something very valuable to you? Many of us have at some point. Several years ago, my wife and I were shopping with our two young sons in a mall in Augusta, Georgia. Suddenly we realized that our three-year-old was gone! He had just been there holding our hand—and he was gone. Immediately we became frantic. We grabbed hold of our five-year-old so we wouldn't loss him and began to backtrack our steps to the toy store we had just left, looking for him. In a frenzy Susan began looking around. Before long, her eyes met those of a mall security officer standing halfway across the mall. He smiled and began walking toward us—and there holding his hand was our son with tears running down his cheeks. Oh, what a relief we felt. We had found our three-year-old son, and he was okay.

As strange as it might sound, when a disciple comes to Jesus, **he loses his life completely in Christ.** Jesus explained this willingness with these words.

> For whoever wants to save his life will lose it, but
> whoever loses his life because of me will save it.
> (Luke 9:24)

This is one of those many places in the gospels where Jesus turned traditional thinking on its head. By stating very similar words several times in the gospels,[73] he leaves us little doubt as to their importance. They bring us to a deep spiritual paradox that many struggle to accept because it contradicts most of what we have been taught by the world. While in the world it seems to be pure foolishness, in the wisdom of Christ, we are to lose our lives for his sake in order to save them. Making accommodations to the world will only endanger our eternity. Only through personal sacrifice for Christ can we honor and serve the One who loved and saved us. Putting his words in terms we can better understand, Jesus is saying the only way we can turn an eternal profit is to give ourselves completely unto him. Plainly stated, we are to live every moment of every day for him. Paul declared that Christ "died for all, so that they who live might no longer live for themselves, but for him who died and rose on their behalf" (2 Corinthians 5:15 NASB). Every day we are to die to self and live for Christ.

This only makes sense as we acknowledge Jesus as Lord of heaven and earth. As Lord of everything, he is not limited by time and space. He is eternal, and everything else we seek in this world is temporal. We come to realize that nothing in this world will last—not our possessions, not our prestige or power, not even our human relationships. Only what we have in Christ will last for all eternity. One day, everything in this world will be destroyed, and God will create a new heaven and a new earth.[74] For this reason, the Lord adds this question to his teaching.

> For what does it benefit someone if he gains the
> whole world, and yet loses or forfeits himself? (Luke
> 9:25)

The implications to the Master's question are unescapable. **Nothing is more important than Jesus Christ**. We could gain everything that the world has to offer—all the money, all the power, all the prestige, all the possessions, all the popularity—but if we do not have a personal relationship with him, we would lose our eternal souls.[75] We might claim we know him; we may do all kinds of good works in his name. We can even shout the gospel from the top of the highest mountain for everyone to hear. But if we do not give him first place in our everyday lives, there is a very real possibility that on the day of judgment we will suffer the eternal loss of everything, as well as our eternal souls.[76]

Boy, this causes me to pause and consider my own life. Are there things or individuals in my life that are more important than Jesus? How about you?

Such was the case in the parable of the rich fool. According to Jesus:

> The land of a rich man produced plentifully, and he thought to himself, 'What shall I do, for I have nowhere to store my crops?' And he said, 'I will do this: I will tear down my barns and build larger ones, and there I will store all my grain and my goods. And I will say to my soul, "Soul, you have ample goods laid up for many years; relax, eat, drink, be merry."'
>
> But God said to him, 'Fool! This night your soul is required of you, and the things you have prepared, whose will they be?' (Luke 12:12–20 ESV)

Like so many, this man piled up great wealth and then imagined all that it could bring in pleasure, status, and fame. But in his search, he forgot God, and he lost everything—even his eternal soul. The Lord's comment about the man was this: "So is the one who lays up treasure for himself and is not rich toward God" (Luke 12:21,

ESV). "One may experience gain in the world, become famous and powerful, but it will not last. Worldly gain means nothing in eternity."[77]

No further comment is necessary, only a question. In your life, are you more focused on the things of this world than you are on Jesus Christ? According to our Lord, that focus will determine your eternal destination.

Look with me at our scripture. In these words, we discover two competing interpretations, both of which apply to humankind, as well as a promise from our Lord to the one who follows him.

> For whoever is ashamed of me and my words, the Son of Man will be ashamed of him when he comes in his glory and that of the Father and the holy angels. (Luke 9:26)

First, with these words **Jesus made an appeal to the unsaved.** The Lord's warning is to those who do not claim to know him as Savior and Lord. One commentator offered this insight: "To be ashamed of Jesus means to be so proud that one wants to have nothing to do with him and with his words."[78] Throughout my nearly forty years of ministry, I have run across individuals who wanted nothing to do with Jesus Christ. Many times, they stubbornly refused to come to Jesus because of their personal pride in their own ability to handle any situation. Quite honestly, they just didn't see that they needed Jesus in their lives.

In the New Testament, we can point to the religious leaders as an example. They knew the law of Moses better than anyone else in all of Israel. As they sought to obey every "jot" and "tittle" of the law, they were the most moral, the most outstanding Jewish citizens in all the land. In fact, they made a public show of excelling in giving to the poor, fasting, and praying.[79] These are the type of people we would like to move into our neighborhood—law-bidding and religious folk. But Jesus said of them, "Unless your righteousness surpasses that of the scribes and Pharisees, you will not enter the kingdom of heaven" (Matthew 5:20 NASB). Just a few days before his crucifixion, Jesus condemned them, saying, "Woe to you, scribes and Pharisees, hypocrites! ... Serpents, brood of vipers! How can you escape being condemned to hell?" (Matthew 23:13–36 NKJV). He explained to his disciples, "I speak to them in parables: Though seeing, they do not see; thought hearing they do not hear or understand" (Matthew 13:13 NIV). Pride in their religious accomplishments prevented the Pharisees from seeing Jesus as the Messiah they had sought for so long. Pride can blind our eyes and dull our hearing also.

I did not really understand Jesus's pronouncement here until a few months ago. My wife and I had gone to a local restaurant for supper. The individual who waited on us was just like this. Although the waiter took our drink order, somehow he became confused and brought what we had not ordered. Throughout our meal, he walked around the dining area as if he was in a fog. When we waved at him and even raised our voices to get his attention, he looked directly at us, but he still did not see us and just kept on going. The one time he stopped by to see how we were doing, we asked for more water, but he never returned with more water. He just disappeared somewhere. And when he took our check to pay for our meal, he never returned with my change. It goes without saying, we have been slow to return to that restaurant. I have never felt so much like I just did not exist. That is how so many people see Jesus—they don't. They are so blind; he does not exist. They are walking around in a fog, totally blind to who Jesus really is. Try as we might, they just cannot hear our witness for Jesus.

By contrast, late one evening another religious leader named Nicodemus came secretly seeking Jesus, saying, "We know that you are a teacher who has come from God." Knowing his greatest need, the Lord said to him, "Ye must be born again ... For God so loved the world, that he gave his one and only Son, so that whoever believes in him shall not perish but have eternal life" (John 3:7, 16

NIV). In other words, Jesus said, "Nicodemus, you need to believe in *Me*." That night, he apparently left unconvinced, but sometime in the days that followed as he continued to watch Jesus and listen to his teaching, I believe Nicodemus was "born again." What is my reason? It is because he came and openly helped Joseph of Arimathea bury Jesus's body after his crucifixion.[80] By touching the dead, both Nicodemus and Joseph became unclean and could not partake of the Passover.[81] Honoring his Master in death had become more important than the Jewish Passover or public opinion. As he buried Jesus, Nicodemus was willing to carry his own cross and denied himself by naming himself as follower of Jesus before the religious leaders. I have no doubt that he was the first among the Sanhedrin to follow Jesus.

Everyone has the same choice to make. Will we choose to come by faith unto Jesus and be saved, or will we reject his invitation to salvation? Jesus told Nicodemus that the failure to make a choice means we have already chosen against Jesus "because they have not believed in the name of God's one and only Son" (John 3:18 NIV). Let me explain this idea in a way that might help you understand.

Just suppose standing before you, I held up a $100 bill and said, "I have a $100 bill for anyone who will come and get it." If you refuse to believe my offer is real and reach to take it, you have chosen not to receive the $100 bill. The same is true about Jesus. If Jesus is speaking to your soul and calling you to salvation, and you refuse to come to him in faith, you have chosen to reject him and the salvation he offers. This is the same choice many people have made. They have chosen to either delay any response to his call to salvation or ignore it altogether; thereby, they have chosen to reject Jesus.

Just a few hours before his crucifixion, Jesus said to His disciples, "I am the way, the truth, and the life. No one comes to the Father except through me" (John 14:6 NKJV). Shortly after the Pentecost, filled with the Spirit, Peter echoed the Lord's words as he said to the Jewish religious leaders, "Salvation is found in no one else, for there is no other name under heaven given to mankind by which we must be saved" (Acts 4:12 NIV).

The Bible is very clear at this point. Jesus is the only way to salvation. The world declares that it does not matter what you believe, as long as you believe in something and live a good life. The Bible tells us that how we live cannot save us, and it does matter what you believe. You must believe in Jesus Christ. He is the only way anyone can find salvation and eternal life. This means that you too have a choice. Will you come to Jesus and follow him as Lord and Savior, or will you reject him? There is no third option.

Furthermore, **a disciple is not ashamed of Jesus.** Look once again at the Savior's words. They also are a warning to everyone who claims to know Christ.

> For whoever is ashamed of me and my words, the Son of Man will be ashamed of him when he comes in his glory and that of the Father and the holy angels. (Luke 9:26)

The Greek *epaischunthē*, the word for "ashamed," introduces the idea "to experience or feel shame or disgrace because of some particular event or activity."[82] Here Jesus implies that there will be times when we become ashamed of him. Just think about this: Are we ashamed of Jesus? John Phillips suggests that Jesus may have had Judas in mind as he uttered these words. He certainly revealed that he was ashamed of the Master as he betrayed him. Maybe it was this hard teaching that first led Judas to consider selling him out to the world.[83] Likewise, Peter was clearly ashamed of Jesus as he denied him while standing around the fire in the courtyard of the high priest.[84] Are we any different? At some point in our lives, have we showed we are ashamed of Jesus by denying him? Moreover, consider this, are we ashamed of His Word? Many appear to be so as they seldom read and often refuse to obey the Bible. The stated truth of scripture is that if we are ashamed of him in this life, Christ will be ashamed of us now and in the life to come.[85] Is this true of your life? Is Christ ashamed of the way you are living your life? Is your life declaring to those who know you: "I am ashamed of Jesus"?

Turn this over in your mind for a moment. Have you ever cringed within yourself when a friend used God's name in vain, and yet you kept your mouth shut? Have you ever kicked yourself after the fact because the opportunity came and you remained silent, rather than tell someone about Jesus? Have you ever felt an urge in your heart to reach out and help someone in Christ's name, but let it pass? If we are honest, every one of us has at some point. We are not all that different from Peter, who was ashamed to be identified with Jesus. In Luke's Gospel we are told that as Peter denied Jesus for the third time, his eyes met the eyes of Jesus. Can you imagine the disappointment and the sadness that showed on his face as Jesus looked at Peter? Immediately, Peter remembered the Lord's prediction, and he ran out of the courtyard and wept bitterly.[86] Peter was ashamed to be identified with Jesus, and in fear he denied him. Are you ashamed to be numbered with Jesus and his followers? Have you denied Jesus?

This brings us to another inescapable question. Is there unconfessed sin in your life? Are you living in disobedience to God's Holy Word? In Galatians, after challenging Christians to "walk by the Spirit," Paul added, "and you will certainly not carry out the desire of the flesh." Then he gave a rather long list of the works of the flesh to warn people about what constitutes sin. At the end of the list, he makes this statement, which is very troubling: "Those who practice such things will not inherit the kingdom of God" (Galatians 5:16–21 NASB). My friends, think about it. Is there sin in your life? As you consider your life, do you fall under these words of condemnation?

In addition, this statement also suggests another question. How do we lovingly make people aware of the consequences of living in sin without sounding condemning, particularly to those who do not want to hear such a warning? As I consider this problem with a heavy heart, seeking some escape from my dilemma, the Spirit reminds me that these are God's words. The Bible is our standard for life—not human wisdom, not public opinion, not some public figure, and not some law of the land. While my personal life should never be a stumbling block before others, the message of the cross is already foolishness to some and a stumbling block to others.[87] My primary task as a minister of the gospel is striving to walk as close to God as I can and make every effort to lovingly proclaim his Word as clearly and accurately as I can—not to make people comfortable in their sin.

Before you become angry at this thought, please consider this. Just suppose your mothers has been diagnosed with cancer. What would you do? Is the answer, anything necessary to save her life? We would go to see the very best cancer specialist we could find. We would make sure she underwent every treatment and took every medication the doctor prescribed. And if she chose to ignore the doctor, we would try to persuade her to reconsider her choices. The goal would be to save her from the death-sentence of cancer.

My friend, the same is true regarding everyone who lives on earth. As a people who believe the Bible, we cannot ignore that it says, "The wages of sin is death" (Romans 6:23 NKJV). This means every one of us is living under not just a physical death sentence but a spiritual death sentence—just as real as cancer. This is the reason we seek to persuade the unsaved to come to Jesus. According to the Bible, it is an urgent matter of life or death. As a Christian, the love of God compels us to share the message of the gospel. This is also the reason we must challenge other believers in their walk with the Lord. As one comes by faith to Jesus, "the old nature has passed away" and the believer can "no longer live in ... sin" (2 Corinthians 5:17–21). In other words, the visible result of salvation is that the one who follows Jesus can no longer continue in sin because he or she is now "dead to sin and alive to God through Christ Jesus" (Romans 6:1–11 NASB).

In John's letter, we find a very similar teaching: "Do not love the world nor the things in the world. If anyone loves the world, the love of the Father is not in him" (1 John 2:15 NASB). Then in the next chapter, he adds:

> Children, let no one deceive you. The one who does what is right is righteous, just as he is righteous. The one who commits sin is of the devil, for the devil has sinned from the beginning. ... This is how God's children and the devil's children become obvious. Whoever does not do what is right is not of God, especially the one who does not love his brother or sister. (1 John 3:7–8, 10)

These and many other passages in the Bible make it clear. If we are not obeying the Bible, we are not obeying God, and we are living in sin. And if we continue to live in sin, we will face God's judgment in the life to come.[88] Or at the very least, we will make it into heaven with the fires of hell nipping at our heels. I do not point this out to condemn anyone but rather to warn of the danger people—good people—face when they ignore God. One unifying teaching of the Bible is that God is a Holy God; and as his children, we are to be holy.[89] Furthermore, because he is holy, the LORD God of heaven and earth hates sin; therefore, sin is punishable by death.[90] But—and please listen to this—God in his love and mercy and grace sent Jesus, who knew no sin to become sin for us,[91] that we might be redeemed from our sin.[92] By dying on the cross, Jesus paid the penalty for our sin[93] so that by grace through faith we might be called the sons of God.[94] But we must come to Jesus and confess our sin and turn from our sin [95]and allow his Spirit to bring forth in us the first fruits of the Spirit.[96] As stated by one author, we must never forget that "to follow the way of the world, instead of the footsteps of Jesus, is to invite the judgment of God."[97]

So once again, is there unconfessed hidden sin in your life that only our Lord knows about? The Bible says all of us are sinners—and that includes even me.[98] This is why everyone needs to come before God Almighty and confess our sin and repent.

Do you remember the promise the apostle John gave us in the first chapter of his letter? "If we confess our sins, He is faithful and just to forgive us our sins and to cleanse us from all unrighteousness" (1 John 1:9 KJV). In confession, we agree with God that we are sinners and acknowledge our sins before him. In repentance, we turn by faith from our sin to Jesus, seeking to live lives that honor and glorify him—and only him. When in confession and repentance we come before him, God forgives and forgets all our sin and gives us salvation and eternal life.

Like the apostle Paul, let us never become ashamed of the gospel of Jesus Christ "for it is the power of God for salvation to everyone who believes" (Romans 1:16 NKJV). Let us stand with Christians down through the centuries with boldness and conviction "that he is able to guard" every promise he has "entrusted" unto us (2 Timothy 1:12 NIV). As we endure the temptations and sufferings of the world, let our confidence be not in ourselves but in the Lord Jesus Christ, "the author and finisher of our faith" (Hebrews 12:2 NKJV).

This leads us to a future promise from the Lord. **Jesus is coming again.** One day "the Son of Man" will come "in his glory and that of the Father and the holy angels." Scripture tells us that when he comes, he will "render every man according to what he has done" (Revelation 22:12 NASB) and separate the faithful sheep from the faithless goats. To the sheep on his right who keep their fealty to him, he will say, "Come, you who are blessed by My Father; inherit the kingdom prepared for you from the foundation of the world." But to the disloyal goats on his left, he shall say, "Depart from me, you cursed … into the everlasting fire prepared for the devil and his angels" (Matthew 25:34, 41 NKJV). The inescapable truth is that only those who maintain their undivided allegiance to him in this life will be rewarded with eternal life. When he comes, we shall live with him; and as his servants, we shall "see his face" and "reign for ever and ever" (Revelation 22:4–5 NIV).

But how do we know this promise is true? Look at the next verse. It is an immediate promise Jesus also made to the disciples.

> Truly I tell you, there are some standing here who will not taste death until they see the kingdom of God. (Luke 9:27)

At first this statement may mystify us. As some suggest, it could point to the triumphant second coming of Christ to establish his kingdom. It could also remind us of the Day of Pentecost as the Spirit came upon the disciples with such power that three thousand souls were saved. But I have come to believe it may have a more immediate context. It is almost as if Jesus is saying, "This is how you may know what I have said is true."

Turn your thoughts to what happened just a few days later. Peter, John, and James went with Jesus on the mountain to pray, and "as he was praying, the appearance of his face changed, and his clothes became dazzling white." "The Greek word *metamorphoō* means "against form." In other words, the Lord Jesus was changed from his present physical form to the glorified body that would be his permanently when he comes to reign on earth."[99] At that moment, Jesus revealed the glory of God, and these three disciples caught a glimpse of the "kingdom of God" through the transfiguration of Jesus. Yet blinded by his humanity, Peter's comment regarding the appearance of Elijah and Moses suggested that the disciples missed the significance of what they were privileged to experience—because both physical and spiritual sleep still filled their eyes. Then, suddenly they heard the voice of God from heaven, saying, "This is my Son, My Chosen One; listen to him!" (Luke 9:28–35 NASB). And in the holy presence of the divine, "they fell face down to the ground and were terrified" (Matthew 17:5–6 NASB). Here the words of the

Master were literally fulfilled. Likewise, we should expect the Lord's warning to "whoever is ashamed of me" to also come to fulfillment.

So how do we escape the chilling judgment of his return? The unsaved person must come confessing his or her sin and turn in faith to Jesus. The believer must return to Jesus in repentance and renew his or her commitment unto the Lord. Once again, for either individual, the key word in following Jesus is "daily." There must be a daily confession of our sin. There must be a daily denial of self. There must be a daily new commitment to Jesus Christ. The only way we can accomplish this is by renewing our relationship with Jesus today ... and renewing it tomorrow ... and the day after that ... and the day after that until we see the coming of our Lord. We are to live in constant, daily surrender to our Lord Jesus Christ. The Bible says, "And now, dear children, continue in him so that when he appears we may have confidence and unashamed before him at his coming" (1 John 2:28 NIV).

Pastor Clifford S. Stewart of Louisville, Kentucky, sent his parents a microwave oven one Christmas. Here's how he recalled the experience:

> They were excited that now they, too, could be a part of the instant generation. When Dad unpacked the microwave and plugged it in, literally within seconds, the microwave transformed two smiles into frowns! Even after reading the directions, they couldn't make it work. Two days later, my mother was playing bridge with a friend and confessed her inability to get that microwave oven even to boil water. "To get this ... thing to work," she exclaimed, "I really don't need better directions; I just needed my son to come along with the gift!"

When God gave the gift of salvation, he didn't send a booklet of complicated instructions for us to figure out; he sent his Son.[100]

All we need to do in response is believe in Jesus Christ as the Son of God. We don't have to understand the whole Bible. We don't ever have to clean our lives up before we answer his call. He accepts us just as we are—warts and all. We simply have to come to him and by faith accept his gift of salvation and allow him to work in and through our lives as we obediently follow him. This brings me once again to the same question: Have you given yourself completely to Jesus?

Food for Thought

In your daily walk with Jesus, have you died to self?

Are you living as if you are ashamed of Jesus? Is there unconfessed sin in your life? Do you seek to obey the Bible?

Have you given yourself completely to Jesus? What hinders you from making this commitment?

As they were traveling on the road someone said to him, "I will follow you wherever you go."

Jesus told him, "Foxes have dens, and birds of the sky have nests, but the Son of Man has no place to lay his head."

Then he said to another, "Follow me."

"Lord," he said, "first let me go bury my father."

But he told him, "Let the dead bury their own dead, but you go and spread the news of the kingdom of God."

Another said, "I will follow you, Lord, but first let me go and say goodbye to those at my house."

But Jesus said to him, "No one who puts his hand to the plow and looks back is fit for the kingdom of God." (Luke 9:57–62)

CHAPTER 3

The Call to Relinquish

As the offering tray passed, a little girl took the tray, put it on the floor, and stood up in the offering plate. The usher said, "Honey, why are you doing that?"

And she said, 'Because they taught me in Sunday school that my whole body was to be offered to the Savior." This little girl got the point that she was the one who belonged in the tray, and that God does not want donations.[101]

Have you place yourself in God's offering plate? How much of yourself are you willing to give to the LORD Jesus Christ? Are you prepared to surrender 10 percent of your life? Fifty percent? One hundred percent? Throughout his earthly ministry, people responded differently to the Lord's call to follow him. Some reacted very positively, while others spurned his call to accompany him along his journey. In God's Word, we read about three individuals and what the Lord required of them if they followed him. From the biblical accounts,[102] we cannot determine whether the people involved followed Jesus or not, although we are left with the distinct impression that they chose not to follow him.

In his book *The Wonderful Spirit Filled Life*, Charles Stanley writes:

In water-safety courses a cardinal rule is never to swim out to a drowning man and try to help him as long as he is thrashing about. To do so is to commit suicide. As long as a drowning man thinks he can help himself, he is dangerous to anyone who tries to help him. His tendency is to grab the one trying to aid him and take them both down in the process. The correct procedure is to stay just far enough away so that he can't grab you. Then you wait. And when he finally gives up, you make your move. At that point the one drowning is pliable. He won't work against you. He will let you help.

The same principle holds true in our relationship with the Holy Spirit. Until we give up, we aren't ready to be helped. We will work against him rather than with him.[103]

At the very heart of following Jesus is the willingness to surrender ourselves completely to him. If we are following him, our lives, our activities, our desires, our words, our thoughts, and a host of other things—which in themselves may not be bad—must not work against the Spirit's influence upon our lives. From the Lord's perspective, we must relinquish everything that keeps us from completely surrendering to him. At its core, discipleship was not a casual affair with the Lord. Nor do we have the option of negotiating more generous terms. The Lord will not compromise his holy commands to fit our desires. Instead, we are to give ourselves completely to him. The simple truth is that total submission is all-important because our outward actions are an indication of our inward relationship to him. They cry out for all to observe if we are his and he is ours.

More specifically, this means that when we follow Jesus, **we are willing to make any sacrifice for him**. According to Matthew's account the man who approached Jesus in our scripture was a scribe,[104] hence a devoted religious man. It also appears that although he said, "Lord, I follow you anywhere you go," in his enthusiasm he failed to understand the implications of following Jesus. He did not see the difficulties, the sacrifice, nor the selfless service involved in such a commitment. But Jesus saw his heart[105] and knew the nature of his faith. And the Lord demanded from him a level of commitment that this scribe man was unable to give. Observe the Lord's words.

> Foxes have dens, and birds of the sky have nests,
> but the Son of Man has no place to lay his head.
> (Luke 9:58)

The sacrifice Jesus mentioned here is the security and comfort that foxes, birds, and other animals naturally enjoy. Foxes have dens for the protection and comfort of their cubs. Birds usually have nests hidden from predatory animals in which to raise their families. But Jesus makes the claim that he had none of these. He had "no place to lay his head." It is difficult for us to imagine having no place to lay our head at night when we lie down to sleep. Most people in the United States, except under unusual circumstances, have protection from nature's elements and predators. We can hide behind the doors of our homes in safety. Within the walls of our homes we find most of the things we consider necessary for comfort and ease. And in our bedrooms, we have at least a semicomfortable bed and more than one pillow on that bed.

As I read this conversation, the image that comes to mind is somewhat different. It is the image I saw in Brazil a few years ago as people living in boxes lined a major highway in Sao Paulo, or as might be seen in certain areas in many of cities in the USA. It is of an individual who lives on the street in a box, a doorway, or maybe a parked car because he or she has no other option. Whether we realize it or not, our Lord was for all intents and purposes homeless. Yes, Peter's home became the hub of his Galilean ministry, and it appears that when they were near Jerusalem, he often stayed with Mary, Martha, and Lazarus in Bethany. But for the most part, Jesus had no real "place to lay his head." He did not have a place that offered the same comfort and security many people around the world enjoy. Please understand that I do not want to equate our Lord to the less desirable characteristics we often attribute to such persons. But Jesus does seem to be saying to those of us who enjoy comfort and security beyond measure that he had none of the things you and I tend to take for granted.

The simple fact is, it was a different time. Things were much more difficult in Bible times for the vast majority of people. Yes, there were wealthy people who enjoyed all the comforts the society of the time could offer. And yes, with the conquest of the region by the Roman Empire many things had begun to change. But for the most part, Jesus and his disciples traveled from place to place on roads that were often little more than dirt cart paths. There were essentially no hotels as we know them in which to spend the night. Like most people, Jesus and his followers had to largely depend upon the kindness of others for lodging. Having limited resources, no doubt they usually had to camp and sleep along the side of the road wrapped up in their cloaks. Maybe for warmth there was even times they huddled together against the elements.

In truth, things in Palestine had not changed very much since the time of Jacob. Genesis tells us that one evening after Jacob fled from home, he took "one of the stones ... put it under his head, and lay down in that place" (Genesis 28:11 NASB). Can you imagine sleeping on the ground using a rock as your pillow when you sleep? Our Lord could; as could his disciples. This apparently was how Jesus spent many nights—because he was always traveling, and there were so few people who were willing to go against the religious establishment and give him a better place to sleep. In the days leading up to this narrative, he had been rejected by Judea,[106] Galilee had cast him out,[107] the people of the Gadarenes had pleaded with him to leave,[108] and most recently Samaritans had refused to give him lodging.[109] [110] So just think about it. Being rejected time after time, the Lord and his followers were often forced to use a rock for a pillow because there was nothing else available. To me this sounds beyond uncomfortable. Regardless of what some may teach, following Jesus is not a casual affair without hardship, sacrifice, and loss.

In a country where we have more comforts than any other people in the world, this idea is extremely difficult for us to understand because we like our comforts. Even when we go camping, our roughing it is to drive our RVs with many of the comforts of home into a campground with running water and electricity and park them. Pressured from every corner, we have determined that there are certain comforts we simply cannot do without. And this list is growing every day. Traditionally necessities for life have been food, clothing and shelter, but most people would add electricity, a bathroom with running water, a soft bed with clean sheets and a warm blanket, central heating and air conditioner, cable or satellite TV, and the list goes on from there. Today, many people, especially young people, would *almost die* without cell phone reception or an internet connection. The sad thing is that on a personal level, many people have allowed these comforts to become more valuable than knowing Jesus Christ. Many people in this nation and around the world have chosen personal comfort over Christ.

Now please understand. Our Master is not asking that we give up all the luxuries of life. (Did I hear a sigh of relief? Let me repeat that.) Jesus is not asking that we give up all our luxuries. Many of the greatest saints throughout time were wealthy men and women. Rather, he is saying, "If you are to follow me, you must be willing 'to lay your head on a stone as your pillow' when that is what the situation demands." In other words, we must be willing to make great personal sacrifices for Jesus, including giving up all our comforts. They must never be so important to us that the luxuries of life endanger our relationship with our heavenly Father. Our luxuries should never prevent us from reaching out and helping others who have greater needs than we might have. Like the widow in the temple, we are not to give out of our surplus but our poverty.[111] Most of those who serve as international missionaries understand this teaching from the Lord. In many countries, they work for low pay, sometimes under what we would consider deplorable conditions with the threat of physical abuse, arrest, or worse as they live among the people they serve and seek to win for Christ. They are willing to do whatever it takes so people might come to know Jesus. Traditionally many church planters, pastors, and their families have also made some of the same sacrifices in order to serve God. When we traveled to Armenia or other foreign lands, we gave up certain comforts—such as American toilets—in order to share the gospel with the people.

The apostle Paul also spoke of his willingness to make sacrifices for the sake of the gospel in his first letter to Corinthians.

> Although I am a free man and not anyone's slave, I have made myself a slave to everyone, in order *to win* more people. To the Jews I became like a Jew, *to win* Jews; to those under the law, like one under the law—though I myself am not under the law—*to win* those under the law. To those who are without the law—though I am not without God's law but under the law of Christ?—*to win* those without the law. To the weak I became weak, in order *to win* the weak. I have become all things to all people, so that I may by every possible means save some. Now I do all this because of the gospel, so I may share in the blessings." (1 Corinthians 9:19–23) [Italics added for emphasis.]

Do you notice the words *to win* were repeated over and over and over? Paul become "a slave" that people might come to Jesus. He was willing to make any sacrifice that people might come to a saving knowledge of Jesus Christ. He was even willing to be "cut off from Christ for the sake of my people," the Israelite people (Romans

9:3 NIV). To Timothy, he said, "I endure everything for the sake of the elect, that they too may obtain the salvation that is in Christ Jesus, with eternal glory" (2 Timothy 2:10 NIV). In his letter to the Philippians he was willing to suffer personally that "Christ is preached. And because of this I rejoice" (Philippians 1:17–18 NIV). No sacrifice was too great if people were brought to saving knowledge of Jesus Christ.

This is the same emphasis Jesus made in our scripture. Our Lord called for his followers to relinquish everything for his kingdom—to be willingly to make any sacrifice for Jesus. This was one of the characteristics of the New Testament church. They were willing to make great personal sacrifices for the cause of Christ. A casual reading of the opening chapters of the book of Acts reveals that they were willing to sell their property and share everything to meet the needs of other believers.[112] They suffered religious persecution and even death for the cause of Christ; and rejoiced in doing so.[113] They were willing to share the master's homelessness and ultimately his rejection and sacrifice on the cross.

Through these words, Jesus is calling us to make the same commitment. We must not permit our comforts—our blessings from God—to prevent us from following him. In other words, we are not to be so tied to our comforts that we refuse to follow him wherever he calls us to go. No sacrifice is too great for the cause of Christ if we are "to win" the lost to Jesus. Maybe as William Barclay suggests, "We have done great hurt to the church by letting people think that church membership need not make so very much difference. We ought to tell them that it should make all the difference in the world. We might have fewer people; but those we had would be really pledged to Christ."[114]

Also, consider this: if we follow Jesus, **he is at the center of our priorities.** As we consider the second man, it is in the realm of possibility that he had overheard the conversation between Jesus and the scribe, so when Jesus addressed him, saying, "Follow Me," he had a ready-made excuse—"First let me to go bury my father" (Luke 9:59).

"The problem here is not burying our relatives. Rather, the problem in this situation is 'me first' attitude seen in the man."[115] He was focused on something other than Jesus. On several occasions, Jesus demanded we make him the number one priority in our lives. In the Sermon on the Mount, he challenged his listeners: "Seek ye first the kingdom of God" (Matthew 6:33 KJV). If we are following Jesus Christ, nothing, even our families, can be more important than him. Following the Lord must be the first consideration in our lives. Knowing and serving him must be our goal in life. This was not true of this man; so Jesus bluntly said to get his attention:

> Let the dead bury their own dead, but you go and spread the news of the kingdom of God." (Luke 9:60)

Before you are offended and stop reading, let's try to understand what the Lord is saying. Yes, according to scripture we are to honor our mothers and fathers.[116] Yes, we are to support them and take care of them in their old age. And, yes, we are to lovingly bury them when God chooses to call them home. All this is a part of life. It is our God-given responsibility. At one point the Lord very bluntly condemned the religious leaders because they had provided for themselves a legal loophole to escape these responsibilities.[117] And lest we forget, Paul also instructed the "children or grandchildren … to show piety at home and to repay their parents, for this is good and acceptable before God." He further stated that if anyone fails to do so, he has denied "the faith and is worse than an unbeliever" (1 Timothy 5:4, 8 NKJV).

Also, understand that Jewish law required the quick burial of the dead—often the same day—followed by a time of mourning.[118] It was a sacred duty of the surviving family. So outwardly it would seem this man made a reasonable request, but this only made the words of Jesus even more demanding. From this perspective, Jesus was demanding that the man leave home before he buried his dead father. In which case, we see that Jesus stipulated complete surrender from those who follow him. On the other hand, some commentators have suggested that his parents were still living.[119] If this was the situation, he was obviously using his parents as an excuse to delay indefinitely surrendering his life to the Lord's call. Don't we sometimes do the same or at least something similar? Putting off things that make us uncomfortable is very common among humankind. All we really know is that by his own words, he wanted to put off making any commitment until he had first buried his parents after an uncertain period. For all we know, his father may have been dead or at the point of death.[120]

Please understood that Jesus is not against funerals and taking time to bury a loved one. Rather, if we take the Lord literally, he was speaking to shock the man into realizing that we must not hesitate in giving him the priority in our lives. There is no more pressing issue in our lives than following Jesus. We should never value any person more than we value the Lord Jesus Christ. "The apostle Paul wrote in the same vein to the Corinthian believers who were troubled about marriage, celibacy, and similar issues: 'I want you to do whatever will help you serve the Lord best, with as few distractions as possible.'" (1 Corinthians 7:35).[121] Admittedly, we are a people who are very easily distracted, especially when we are asked to do something we really don't want to do. None of us want to give up anything on this earth, especially family.

One thing we do know—God is all-knowing. By coming in human flesh, Jesus shows us just how far he is willing to go to assure us that he understands the circumstances of our lives. He loves us despite our fickleness. He sees into our hearts and knows our deepest desires. The Lord knows there are times our desire to follow him is hindered by personal fears and weakness. He knows even before we utter a word whether our excuses are based on fact or fiction. We might deceive others, but we can never mislead him. And although our actions hurt, he still loves us even in our inconsistency. His death and resurrection show us that his eternal passion is that we might know and love him as he knows and loves us. This will be fulfilled only as we spend eternity in his presence.

In addition, there is another side of the issue we must consider. Sometimes our God calls us to what seems an impossible level of commitment—in order to test our commitment to him. This is what God did as he asked Abraham to sacrifice Isaac on the mountain. God was testing Abraham (and Sarah) to see how committed he was to the LORD God.[122] Abraham passed the test with flying colors, but would we?

This truth must be always before us. How we response to his call reveals the exact nature of our commitment to him. When Jesus calls, he is calling for a radical change in the priorities of our lives. We are to relinquish everything for Him. This means completely reordering our lives according to his plan and not attempting to get him to alter his plans to match ours. He is God; as such, he knows what is best for us. Our commitment to the Lord Jesus Christ must take precedence over all other commitments that worldly traditions would place on us. We should never make him settle for second place in our lives. Furthermore, no sacrifice should be too great for the cause of Jesus Christ. Our priorities—how we spend our time and money, what we talk about, where we go, what we do, whom we spend time with—speak volumes about how much we love the Lord. Since we live in a "me first" society, we must continually ask ourselves, "Does Jesus occupy first place in my life? Am I giving him my all?" Don't wait until a better time to follow and serve him. When he calls, follow him immediately.

Please allow me to pause at this point for just a moment. We must also recognize that Jesus is not calling us to be active in his kingdom's work just for activities' sake. We should never make religious activity a priority in our lives. This was a big part of the Pharisees' religion. They sought public recognition through very strict but meaningless public activity. In other words, we should never go, go, go just because "this is what a Christian does," or to receive personal recognition. To do so is to make religious activity an idol. Instead, we must be about our heavenly Father's work, always focused upon his will for our lives. When good activities, even going to church, become important as a matter of show—"Look what I'm doing"—then it becomes self-serving. It becomes idolatry. This was at least part of what Jesus was talking about in the Sermon on the Mount regarding praying on the street corner or the giving alms to the poor or fasting.[123] We must never be like the Jewish religious leaders and seek earthly praise for our good works. Our focus must be to "let your light so shine before men, that they may see your good works and glorify your Father in heaven" (Matthew 5:16 NKJV).

In *Christian Living*, Lafcadio Hearn tells of a Japanese seashore village over a hundred years ago, where an earthquake startled the villagers one autumn evening. But being accustomed to earthquakes, they soon went back to their activities. Above the village on a high plain, an old farmer was watching from his house. He looked at the sea, and the water appeared dark and acted strangely, moving against the wind, running away from the land. The old man knew what it meant. His one thought was to warn the people in the village.

He called to his grandson, "Bring me a torch! Make haste!" In the fields behind him lay his great crop of rice. Piled in stacks ready for the market, it was worth a fortune. The old man hurried out with his torch. In a moment the dry stalks were blazing. Then the big bell pealed from the temple below: fire!

Back from the beach, away from the strange sea, up the steep side of the cliff, came the people of the village. They were coming to try to save the crops of their rich neighbor. "He's mad!" they said.

As they reached the plain, the old man shouted back at the top of his voice, "Look!" At the edge of the horizon they saw a long, lean, dim line—a line that thickened as they gazed. That line was the sea, rising like a high wall and coming more swiftly than a kite flies. Then came a shock, heavier than thunder. The great swell struck the shore with a weight that sent a shudder through the hills and tore their homes to matchsticks. It drew back, roaring. Then it struck again, and again, and yet again. Once more it struck and ebbed; then it returned to its place.

On the plain no word was spoken. Then the voice of the old man was heard, saying gently, "That is why I set fire to the rice." He stood among them almost as poor as the poorest, for his wealth was gone—but he had saved four hundred lives by the sacrifice.[124]

My friends, when we follow Jesus, no sacrifice can be too great. Just as in this story, there are lives at stake. Our lives must be aligned with the priorities of the Lord. Just as he came to seek and save the lost,[125] we are to seek the lost and tell them about the Savior. If Jesus has first place in our lives, his goals will become our goals, and we must treasure him above everything and everyone.

Finally, when we follow Jesus, **we are focused on the kingdom of God.** A third man approached the Lord and said, "I will follow you, Lord, but first let me go and say goodbye to those at my house." Even Elijah permitted Elisha to say goodbye to his parents.[126] But knowing this man's reluctance, the Lord dismissed his divided devotion and called for an even higher level of commitment, saying,

> No one who puts his hand to the plow and looks
> back is fit for the kingdom of God. (Luke 9:62)

Anyone who has ever plowed a field knows that it is impossible to plow a straight line if one is constantly looking back over one's shoulder. To plow a straight line, we must constantly focus our eyes ahead of us. We pick some object ahead of us—a post or a tree—as a goal and push the plow straight toward that goal. The same is true with following Jesus. We must freely cut ties with the past and keep our eyes on the goal he has established for us. We can't keep looking back at what was in the past, what we have given up, what might have been, or what has changed. If we do, we will wander from God's plan and purpose for our lives, only to discover we have wandered far from his path.

Lest we forget, Lot's wife was told to run to the mountains and not look back, but she could not resist the temptation, and looking back at the destruction of Sodom she became a pillar of salt.[127] Throughout the exodus, the Jewish people were constantly looking back at their days in Egypt as slaves and incorrectly seeing them as better days. Reading the biblical accounts, it becomes evident that their complaining eventually led to rebellion and punishment by God. I mention these examples to offer a word of caution. They give notice of the danger one faces when a person takes his or her eyes from the divinely appointed goal. It can only lead an individual into much heartache and even destruction. There will always be seemingly good excuses to not follow Jesus. We must relinquish the right to look over our shoulder at the past.

William W. Borden was the heir of a wealthy Chicago family. In 1904 and 1905, at the age of eighteen, he traveled around the world. This was followed by a brilliant education at Yale and then Princeton Seminary, where he committed his life to seek to win the Muslims in China to Christ. Before he left, Borden gave away some $500,000 (equivalent to $10 million in the 1990s [probably several times more than that by now]) and served at the age of twenty-three as a trustee of Moody Bible Institute. In 1913, in his twenty-sixth year, he left for Egypt and never looked back. It was the final year of his life, because in Cairo he contracted cerebral meningitis. As he lay dying, he scribbled this note: "No reserve, no retreat, no regrets." That is the kind of attitude Christ was calling for here in the ninth chapter of Luke.[128]

We must keep our eyes forward on the kingdom of God. We ought to keep our focus on the road that lies before us as we follow our Lord. The apostle Paul said, "Brothers and sisters, I do not consider myself yet to have taken hold of it. But one thing I do: Forgetting what is behind and straining toward what is ahead, I press on toward the goal to win the prize for which God has called me heavenward in Christ Jesus" (Philippians 3:13–14 NIV).

With all that is in us, we are to strive daily to reach the kingdom of God. Nothing should lead us from that path. What did Jesus say? "Seek you first the kingdom of God and His righteousness, and all these things will be added unto you" (Matthew 6:33 NKJV). A kingdom is where a king rules and reigns. Jesus Christ is the King of kings and Lord of lords. He is the Creator of heaven and earth. The heavenly Father has given him all authority.

In the prophetic vision of Daniel, we read:

> I saw in the night visions, and behold,
> with the clouds of heaven there came one like a son
> of man,
> and he came to the Ancient of Days
> and was presented before him.
> And to him was given dominion and glory and a
> kingdom,
> that all peoples, nations, and languages should
> serve him;
> his dominion is an everlasting dominion,
> which shall not pass away,
> and his kingdom one that shall not be destroyed.
> (Daniel 7:13–14 ESV)

Jesus unequivocally stated to his disciples, "All authority has been given to me in heaven and earth ... I am with you always, to the end of the age" (Matthew 20:18, 20). Under the divine inspiration of the Holy Spirit, Paul declared because of what Jesus accomplished on the cross:

> Therefore God has highly exalted him
> and bestowed on him the name that is above every
> name,

so that at the name of Jesus every knee should bow,
in heaven and on earth and under the earth,
and every tongue confess that Jesus Christ is Lord,
to the glory of God the Father. (Philippians 2:9–
11 ESV)

Heaven and earth belong to Jesus Christ. This world is his Kingdom, even though he has allowed Satan for a moment in time to deceive himself and claim it as his own. One day in the not so distant future, Jesus will reclaim what is his and destroy the forces of the devil as they are thrown into the lake of fire where they will suffer eternal punishment.[129] Until that day, following our Lord's example, we are to declare to the world the coming of the kingdom of heaven where he will reign forever and ever. As his children, we must cry out with an apology to no one, "Repent, for the kingdom of heaven has come near" (Matthew 4:17 NKJV). Like the apostle Paul, we are to declare without compromise "Jesus Christ and him crucified" (1 Corinthians 2:2 NKJV). To do otherwise is to permit the hundreds, maybe thousands of people we encounter during our time on earth to face divine judgment unprepared for its consequences.[130]

But this is what many Christians have refused to do. With very little visible difference from the Pharisees of the New Testament, we have turned our focus toward accumulating wealth or protecting a position of power. Maintaining tradition and our way of life has become our chief goal. Bearing fruit for the glory of God has become bearing fruit for ourselves in personal acclaim and praise. As true followers of Christ, we must once again make the proclamation of the gospel our principal aim in everything. This goal must govern our every thought and activity in our churches, as well as in our lives. We can no longer afford to focus upon ourselves in order to please ourselves. We must follow the Lord's high purpose of seeking the lost so they might hear the message of salvation. We must make every effort to proclaim, "Repent for the Kingdom of God is at hand" (Matthew 4:17 NKJV)—if we are to be fit for the kingdom. We must fall before Jesus, the King of heaven and earth and confess our sin, and in repentance return to the task of declaring Jesus to a lost world. We must once again value the coming kingdom of God over against anything or anyone. Jesus Christ must be first in our lives. This means renouncing everything for the cause of Jesus Christ.

One Haitian pastor illustrates the need for total commitment to Christ with this parable:

A certain man wanted to sell his house for $2,000. Another man wanted very badly to buy it, but because he was poor, he couldn't afford the full price. After much bargaining, the owner agreed to sell the house for half the original price with just one stipulation: he would retain ownership of one small nail protruding from just over the door.

After several years, the original owner wanted the house back, but the new owner was unwilling to sell. So first the owner went out, found the carcass of a dead dog, and hung it from the nail he still owned. Soon the house became unlivable, and the family was forced to sell the house to the owner of the nail.

The Haitian pastor's conclusion: "If we leave the devil with even one small peg in our life, he will return to hang his rotting garbage on it, making it unfit for Christ's habitation."[131]

Have you left a peg in your life that Satan uses to prevent you from being used of God? If we are willing to sacrifice our comforts … if we make Jesus the priority in our lives … if we are focused on God's kingdom … our lives will be blessed beyond imagination because like the little girl we talked about earlier—we have placed ourselves in God's offering plate. Discipleship involves sharing in our Lord's commitment, making personal sacrifices and suffering for the cause of Christ.

Bruce Thielemann tells the story of a church elder who showed what it means to follow Jesus.

A terrible ice storm had hit Pittsburgh, making travel almost impossible. At the height of the storm, a church family called their pastor about an emergency. Their little boy had leukemia, and he had taken a turn for the worse. The hospital said to bring the boy in, but they could not send an ambulance, and the family did not own a car.

The pastor's car was in the shop, so he called a church elder. The elder immediately got in his car and began the treacherous journey. The brakes in his car were nearly useless. It was so slick that he could not stop for stop signs or stop lights. He had three minor accidents on the way to the family's house.

When he reached their home, the parents brought out the little boy wrapped in a blanket. His mother got in the front seat and held her son, and the father got in the back. Ever so slowly they drove to the hospital. Says Thielemann:

> They came to the bottom of a hill and as they managed to skid to a stop, he tried to decide whether he should try to make the grade on the other side, or whether he should go to the right and down the valley to the hospital. And as he was thinking about this, he chanced to look to the right and he saw the face of the little boy. The youngster's face was flushed, and his eyes wide with fever and with fear. To comfort the child, he reached over and tousled his hair. Then it was that the little boy said to him, "Mister, are you Jesus?" Do you know in that moment he could have said yes. For him to live was Jesus Christ.

People who piddle around with life never know moments like that.

Loving as Jesus loved requires courage.[132]

While in my late-teens, I sang at times with both the youth and adult choirs in my home church. Although the title of the musical escapes my memory, the opening words and the musical score of one song have stayed with me down through the years. Based upon the apostles Paul's words to the Galatians,[133] they read:

I am crucified with Christ,
nevertheless I live,
yet not I, not I,
but Christ liveth in me.
Christ liveth in me.[134]

Is this a statement about your life? Have you given yourself completely to Jesus? Like the little girl in the story at the beginning of this chapter, have you given yourself as an offering unto the Savior? Are you following the LORD Jesus Christ with all your being?

Food for Thought

Have you given everything to Jesus—your job, your money, your time, your friends, your wife and children, and your life?

Take a moment to think, what have you kept back from Jesus Christ? Why?

Is Jesus Christ and his kingdom the number one priority in your life?

Are you telling others about Jesus?

Now great crowds were traveling with him. So he turned and said to them: "If anyone comes to me and *does not hate* his own father and mother, wife and children, brothers and sisters—yes, and even his own life—he cannot be my disciple. "Whoever *does not bear* his own cross and come after me cannot be my disciple.

"For which of you, wanting to build a tower, doesn't first sit down and calculate the cost to see if he has enough to complete it? Otherwise, after he has laid the foundation and cannot finish it, all the onlookers will begin to ridicule him, saying, 'This man started to build and wasn't able to finish.' Or what king, going to war against another king, will not first sit down and decide if he is able with ten thousand to oppose the one who comes against him with twenty thousand? If not, while the other is still far off, he sends a delegation and asks for terms of peace. "In the same way, therefore, every one of you who *does not renounce* all his possessions cannot be my disciple.

"Now, salt is good, but if salt should lose its taste, how will it be made salty? It isn't fit for the soil or for the manure pile; they throw it out. Let anyone who has ears to hear listen" (Luke 14:26–35) [Italic added for emphasis.].

CHAPTER 4

The Call to Count the Cost

Thanksgiving is one of my favorite times of the year. Yes, you guessed it. One of the reasons I like Thanksgiving is the great feast we enjoy around the big dining room table. Spread out on the bar and counters are turkey and dressing, mashed potatoes, biscuits and gravy, green bean casserole, broccoli casserole, sweet potato casserole, deviled eggs, pumpkin and apple pie, a fruit salad and several delicious cakes. There is always so much food one can't get it all on a plate. And then, just think about all the family members and friends who gather around the tables that have been set up for everyone to eat this great festive meal. My mouth just waters to think about all that food. (What can I say? I like turkey and dressing!) My heart beats harder when I consider all that are gathered around. My thoughts and prayers turn to the Lord in thanksgiving for all his bountiful blessings.

The Lord Jesus Christ once told a story about an even greater supper.[135] Invitations had already been sent out days ahead of time to all the guests, but as the day for the banquet arrived, several individuals offered excuses and refused to attend. The first man declined to go so he could look at a piece of land he had just purchased. The second thought it was more important to try out his new oxen. The third person asked to be excused to be with his new wife. Angered by their rejection, the host sent his servants to invite others, saying, "Not one of those who were invited will get a taste of my banquet" (Luke 14:24 NIV). The spiritual implication is clearly that because these people rejected the Master, they too will be rejected by him.

It was with this background that Jesus turned to the multitude gathered before him and made a statement regarding discipleship that at first reading, seems to be some of the most disturbing words ever uttered by our Lord. They are deeply troubling because they appear to contradict much of what we have been taught since childhood.

Paying the Price

A little girl came to her father and asked him for a nickel. The father reached into his pocket, but he didn't have any change. All he had was a twenty-dollar bill. He knew that was a lot of money, but he figured that his daughter had been a good girl. He decided to give her the twenty.

The little girl said, "Oh no, Daddy. You don't understand. I want a nickel."

"No, honey, you don't understand. This is a bunch of nickels. This is a twenty-dollar bill."

But the little girl didn't understand. She said, "Daddy, why won't you give me a nickel?"

He tried to explain. He tried to tell her how many nickels were in a dollar, and how many dollars were in a twenty-dollar bill. She wasn't getting it. So she started crying and having a temper tantrum. "Daddy, you said you were going to give me a nickel. Why won't you give me a nickel?"

That's exactly what we do. We settle for a nickel when God offers us twenties.[136]

Too often when we follow Jesus, we set our goals too low. We try to do just enough to get inside heaven's gate, and we miss the even greater blessings God wishes to freely give us. We tend to forget that "there is a difference between claiming to be a Christian and being a disciple of Jesus Christ. 'Disciple' means 'disciplined one'—one who is committed to the cause of the kingdom."[137] By failing to recognize this distinction, we keep our aim low and compromise the truth of the gospel. The result is that we never truly experience the fullness of the Holy Spirit's presence in our lives. But Jesus wants us to settle for nothing less than the best. His greatest desire is to bless everyone who follows him, especially those who are willing to pay the price for following him.

This means that **Jesus is to be the number one priority in our lives.** In the passage under consideration, did you happen to notice the first reason given by the Lord for why we "cannot be his disciples"? It's troubling, isn't it? It disturbs us because as stated by Jesus, we are to "hate" those individuals we have always been taught to love the most—our "father and mother, wife and children, brothers and sisters—yes, and [our] own life." Surely these words must have caused quite a stir among his listeners as well.

Among the many things we first learn as a child is that the members of our family are to be cherished and valued above everything else. No one or nothing else is to be more important in our lives than these individuals. The fifth commandment tells us to "honor your father and your mother" (Exodus 20:12). In Proverbs, King Solomon encouraged his son, saying, "Listen, my son, to your father's instruction, and do not forsake your mother's teaching" (Proverbs 1:8 NIV). In his letter to the Ephesians, the apostle instructed: "Husbands, love your wives, just as Christ also loved the church and gave Himself for her." Paul then added a few verses later, "Children, obey your parents in the Lord for this is right. Honor your father and mother" (Ephesians 5:25; 6:1–2). Honor and love within the family has always been a hallmark of a wholesome society. Fathers and mothers love their sons and daughters. Children honor and love their parents. Husbands and wives honor, respect, and love one another. So why did Jesus suggest a departure from this historical biblical standard?

In a parallel account we find these words: "The one who loves a father or mother more than me is not worthy of me; the one who loves a son or daughter more than me is not worthy of me" (Matthew 10:37). So obviously there is a greater principle involved here. Since God never contradicts himself, in this case we are not to take the words of Jesus literally and "hold malice or bitterness or anger toward our families."[138] Instead, as God's children, love should always rule our lives. Here the Master Storyteller is using a biblical idiom that means to "love less."[139] He is addressing our most definitive argument against following the Lord—our families. Once again, speaking in the extreme, the Master is making a very important point. In essence, he is saying to those who may seek to follow him:

> "Do you fancy yourself a disciple? Do you think you are going to follow me? Well then, you must love me so much more that your love for your family seems like hatred in comparison! Hate your own life. Otherwise, don't pretend to be following me."[140]

To the world such words are astonishing. Jesus is calling his followers to stop pretending they are following him. We are not to be divided in our loyalties or half-hearted in our efforts to follow him. Instead, we are to love, cherish, and value him even more than we love, cherish, and value our own flesh and blood. In other words, "our love for him must be so great that our natural love for our family pales in comparison."[141] You are to love the Lord Jesus Christ "with all your heart, and with all your soul, and with all your mind and with all your strength" (Mark 12:30 NASB). Our relationship with Jesus Christ is to be the number one priority in our lives.

Take a moment and think about it. If your career, playing or watching sports, attaining wealth, even spending time with your family or friends is more important than Jesus, are you really following him? Nothing and no one else can be more important to us than the Lord Jesus Christ.

So why is this so important?

The reasons are simple. To begin with, we must understand that our heavenly Father's love for us is without match. Yes, our parents, mates, and children love us, but God loves us more. In fact, he loved us before we were even born into the world he created. He loved us enough to send Jesus, his one and only Son, into the world to die on a cross that we might have eternal life.[142] The apostle Paul expressed the Lord's sacrifice this way: "For you know the grace of our Lord Jesus Christ, that though he was rich, yet for your sake he became poor, so that you through his poverty might become rich" (2 Corinthians 8:9 NIV). The simple true is that by coming into this world Jesus Christ gave up everything including the glory of heaven to die on a cross that you might experience the fullness of his love. As hard as it is to grasp, he showed us his great love toward us while we were still living in rebellion and sin against him.[143] The Beloved Apostle John expressed God's unrivaled love in this way:

> God is love. This is how God showed his love among us: He sent his one and only Son into the world that we might live through him. ... He loved us and sent his Son as an atoning sacrifice for our sins. (1 John 4:8–10 NIV)

Also, Jesus is the very essence of God's unconditional love expressed toward all humankind. As Jesus came into this world to walk among us, God in his grace took the initiative to bring us back into a loving relationship with him. Through the Lord's sinless life,[144] Jesus revealed his ability to overcome the same temptations and sin we face every day. By his death on the cross, God disclosed his unsurpassed longing to forgive, redeem, and cleanse us from all sin. In the Lord's resurrection from the tomb, the LORD God displayed his unrivaled power to conquer death and the grave—and hence, redeem us from our sin and grant us eternal life. When Jesus died and arose, the heavenly Father unveiled his ageless loving desire for an eternal relationship with us, beginning first on earth and then reaching throughout all eternity. Through his resurrection, we are transformed into new creatures[145] and are raised to newness of life in him and are justified before God.[146] As we believe in Jesus Christ, we receive forgiveness for our sin and the living hope of eternal life. By faith in him, based upon what Christ accomplished on the cross, we can now stand before God just if we have never sinned.[147] As he died on the cross, Jesus bought us with his own life from the power of sin[148]—so we might experience the fullness of his love.

In addition, while our relationships with family members are of the uttermost importance, they are also temporal. But as we come by faith to Jesus Christ, our personal relationship with him is eternal. Family relationships are earthly; but as his follower, our relationship with Jesus reaches beyond this world into heaven's eternity. Our time with family members is for only sixty, seventy, or for a blessed few, eighty years or more; but at some point, death will separate us from those we love in this life. This is the nature of being human. This is the result of Adam and Eve's refusal to heed God's warning regarding the fruit of the tree of the knowledge of good and evil.[149] In disobedience to God, they ate of the forbidden fruit—and sin and death entered the world. But when we come by faith to Jesus Christ, our sins are forgiven forever, and we become children of the eternal heavenly Father. Death will still reign over this mortal body, but at our physical deaths, our immortal souls will be with God the Father forever and ever.[150] According to the apostle Paul, not even physical death can separate us from the love of God that is in Christ Jesus.[151]

Finally, at different times, for different reasons, our family members will fail us, but Jesus will never betray our trust. He will never fail us. He is faithful and completely dependable. While it may be true that our mothers and fathers will do anything to show us their love and make our lives better, their resources and abilities are limited. Being human, our mates and children can never actually meet all our needs—no matter how hard they may try. But God by his very nature has no such limitations. His resources know no boundaries; they are without measure. He is the Creator of everything; therefore, he knows everything about us—even down to the number of hairs on our heads.[152] Out of his limitless and unconditional love, God's desires for us are far beyond anything any human can provide for us—even those individuals who are the closest to us. In other words, as important as our family relationships may be, they are at best a faint shadow of what we will experience in God's eternal presence; therefore, Jesus must be given first place in our lives. Won't you come by faith to Jesus?

But my friends, please also consider this interesting fact. If our mothers and fathers, wives and children, and sisters and brothers have also come to believe in Jesus and surrender their lives unto him, they too will experience his loving cleansing and spend eternity in his presence. For this reason, after death has visited us on this earth, we will see them all once again in heaven's glory; therefore, we must also tell them about Jesus.

Major General Jeb Stuart expressed his commitment to General Robert E. Lee with a simple salutation on his letters. He would always sign his letters to the commanding general of the Confederacy: "Yours to count on." That should be our daily prayer to our Lord.[153] Likewise, by our commitment to Jesus we are saying, "Lord, you can count on me!"

The simple truth is, **we are to commit our lives completely to Jesus.** Look once again at the Lord's words.

> "Whoever does not bear his own cross and come
> after me cannot be my disciple." (Luke 14:27)

Today, we have washed all the blood from the cross and made it a trinket we wear around our necks. Lest we forget, the cross was one of the most horrifying instruments of death ever devised to execute another human being. It was specifically designed to publicly degrade, torture, and punish a convicted criminal in the cruelest way possible. It was so disgraceful that even the Bible declared, "he who is hanged [on a tree] is accurse of God" (Deuteronomy 21:23 NKJV). So many individuals were crucified through the years by Rome that most soldiers soon become hardened to the task, with some becoming very adept in the cruelty of killing people. Sadly, such inhuman treatment also extended among the masses, as any crucifixion became a form of entertainment. "Only twenty-four years previously, about A.D. 6, 'the Romans crucified hundreds of followers of the rebel, Judas the Gaulonite'"[154] as a visible warning of what happens to all criminals within the empire. Jesus did not need to warn the people about the horror of the cross. They had witnessed it firsthand. It was entirely possible as the Lord spoke these words, they were passing the body of a dead individual still hanging on a cross days after his crucifixion.

My friends, when a person was crucified, no mercy was shown to him. There is absolutely nothing loving about hanging naked on a cross usually for several days exposed to the elements, as well as wild animals and scavenger birds. Meanwhile, the individual was bleeding from appalling open wounds that attracted all types of flies and other insects. In addition, the one on the cross experienced horrible, unending pain from the nails driven into his hands and feet. Hanging on the cross caused unbelievable pain as one's shoulders are pulled out of their joints. Moreover, the position of the individual leaves him fighting for every breath from the increased pressure on his diaphragm. Many times, people died from suffocation rather than the loss of blood. In brief, the cross was an instrument of public humiliation and torture used to kill another individual in the worst way imaginable. It was so horrible that it had been declared that no Roman citizen could ever be crucified.

In contrast, for the follower of Christ the cross serves as a reminder of the sacrifice Jesus made on our behalf at Calvary. He took upon himself the punishment we so richly deserve as he became sin for us that we might be forgiven all our sin. The cross shows us the length God would go to announce his love for all humankind.[155] But it also declares how much a holy God hates sin. It cries out that all sin must be punished. It reminds us that as Jesus Christ died on the cross for us, he freely took upon himself the punishment we rightly desire because we have chosen to sin against a holy and righteous God. Carrying our cross, means we identify daily "with Christ in shame, suffering, and surrender to God's will."[156] As we bear our own cross, we die "to self, to our own plans and ambitions" "in order that others can be saved, helped, redeemed, restored."[157] There is within us a willingness to make sacrifices for the cause of Jesus Christ[158]—even to the point of dying for him.[159] As difficult as this idea may be to accept, if Christ is the first in our lives, we soon discover that no sacrifice is too great for our Lord's sake—even in the arena of family relationships.

The story is told that when James Calvert went out as a missionary to the cannibals of the Fiji Islands, the captain of the ship that had carried him there sought to turn him back by saying, "You will lose your life and the lives of those with you if you go among such savages." Calvert's reply well demonstrates the cost of commitment: "We died before we came here."[160]

My brother and sister in Christ, what price are you willing to pay? There is no higher price than to die for Jesus.

Paying the Price for Trusting Jesus

Many a basketball player has dreamed of having the ball in the closing seconds of a big game and being called on to take the winning shot. What a rush as the seconds tick off the clock. Finding an ever so slight opening, the player leaps in the air and releases the shot over the opponent's outstretched hand just before the buzzer goes off, and the ball swishes through the net. What a thrill the shooter feels as he jumps for joy and high-fives with his teammates.

But what brought that player to this point? It was years of playing games against other prayers who were many times better players. It was thousands of shots, most of which refused to go in and even missed the goal altogether. It was a never-ending devotion to practice and still more practice. It was the blood, sweat, and tears of hard work and repetition and still more repetition. It was a willingness to pay the price to become not just a good player but the best player possible.

Following Jesus is not much different. There is a price to be paid. It involves a lifelong devotion to the Lord Jesus Christ. Just as an athlete knows the price he or she must pay to be the best, there is a price Christians must pay to follow Jesus. But for many in the world of athletics as well as Christianity the price is too high, and we settle for something less than the best.

My brothers and sisters, **we are to count the cost of our commitment to Jesus.** As he spoke, Jesus pointed to a builder who was weighing whether he had the money to build a tower and a king who was wondering if he could defeat his enemy who had a much larger army. Both men were carefully considering their options before they acted—for fear of finding the task more than they can accomplish. The principal difference between the two examples is that the first had a choice of whether to build a tower or not, based on his resources. Meanwhile the king is facing a dilemma that is beyond his control. An enemy is coming against him with twice as many soldiers. The only choice he had to determine was whether to fight a numerically superior force when victory is extremely unlikely or try to negotiate peace with his enemy.

When the two illustrations are considered together, both remind us to consider the cost we may pay for following Jesus. Not one of us wants to pay more than necessary for anything. We usually chose the way that will cost the least, but therein lies much of our problem. Too often we allow the perceived cost to obscure our understanding of the Lord's words, thus permitting it to become an excuse to ignore him. How many times have we counted the cost and found it too high, too steep, or too demanding? This may result in becoming so cautious that we refuse to follow the LORD Jesus Christ.

Consider for a moment the Israelites' actions during the days of the Exodus.[161] At their request,[162] God allowed them to send twelve spies into the Promised Land. Although those men were able to establish that the land was all God promised it would be and much more, ten of the spies emphasized the difficulties facing them. God's promises regarding the land and its inhabitants were completely ignored. Allowing their fears to subdue their faith, in disbelief the Jewish people refused to enter the land. Despite the protest by Caleb and Joshua, they came to believe the cost of conquering the Promised Land would be too high, even though God had promised to go before them.[163] But also understand this—if I read the scripture right—God had essentially already given them the land.[164] They just had to take possession. Ignoring God's faithfulness throughout the Exodus and drowning in dread and fear, they rejected God and even considered returning to Egypt.[165] In his wrath, God condemned the entire nation to wander in the wilderness for forty years because they rejected him as they refused to believe in his promise.

Isn't this how we often respond to God? God has promised to be with us and to supply our every need, but we still permit our fears to control us to the point we refuse to follow him. As we allow our imagination and emotions to control our lives, we miss so many of the blessings God wishes to bestow upon us. Our fears lead us to disobey God and ignore his promises. Concerns over perceived problems and trials become more important than divine guarantees.

Just think about it for a moment. What if, in Genesis,[166] Noah had allowed the cost of following God's command to adversely influence his decision? Would he have built the ark? Several times the Bible says "Noah ... found grace in the eyes of the Lord." That he "was a just man, perfect in his generations. Noah walked with God." We are told that "Noah did; according to all God had commanded him" (Genesis 6:8, 9, 22 NKJV). As he followed God, it just makes sense that during the hundred years it took to build the ark, Noah must have heard more than once what a fool he was for believing God was going to punish the whole world with a flood. Oh, by the way, "What is rain?" some the people may have asked, since there is a possibility they had never seen it before.[167] In sport, they probably mocked him, saying how dumb he was to build an enormous boat on dry land and so far from a large body of water. How stupid he was to believe in a God that did not exist. And even if he did exist, how crazy Noah was to suggest that a loving God would punish everyone on the earth. After all, they were good people just having a good time, not sinners living in rebellion to God. How looney he was to devote his life to such a foolish and useless task. And yet, Noah believed God and "did according to all the Lord had command him" (Genesis 7:5 NKJV).

Yes, I believe Jesus is calling upon us to count the cost of any action we undertake for him. Abraham knew the danger but in faith he willingly paid the price as he left his father and followed God into an unknown land.[168] Then he allowed Lot to take the best pastureland along the Jordan River. Abraham trusted God as he moved into the wilderness of Canaan.[169] In similar fashion, Moses trusted God as he returned to Egypt, a land he had fled forty years earlier, to lead the Israelite nation from captivity to the Promised Land.[170] Moreover, Joshua believed God as he led the Israelite nation to conquer the Promised Land.[171] Surely as they stood before King Nechadnezzar, Shadrach, Meshach, and Abed-nego fully understood the consequences of their commitment to God.[172] Likewise, Daniel understood he had enemies in King Darius's court and that he would end up in the lion's den if he continued to pray three times a day.[173] As did Paul as he boldly stood before the religious leaders and the Roman officials and defended his relationship with God.[174] The same is true of every person throughout the history of the church who has maintained the conviction that Jesus is Lord as he or she faced persecution and possible death.

"Part of the problem in counting the cost is that often we do not know ahead of time what the real cost will be."[175] For instance, going into gospel ministry may mean one's family does without some of the things other members of the congregation enjoy, due to one's income. In addition, one may be forced to confront another individual concerning some activity that is displeasing to God.[176] Missing family gatherings and events may be a part of the cost one pays for following Jesus. Such unpredictable things can bring great hardship. The simple truth is that the choices of discipleship are seldom easy. Regardless the circumstance, counting the cost of following Jesus should never make us so fearful that we surrender to the world's pressure and our personal fears. We too must be mindful of the cost of following Jesus Christ.

Nineteenth century evangelist Dwight L. Moody once said, "There are thousands of men who would become more useful in God's kingdom if they would wake up to this fact: it isn't brains God wants—it is the heart."[177] It is from within the heart that we follow by faith the LORD Jesus Christ no matter what life may bring our way.

In the first chapter of 2 Corinthians, Paul was sharing in broad terms some of the things that had happened in his life.

> For we do not want you to be unaware, brothers, of the affliction we experienced in Asia. For we were so utterly burdened beyond our strength that we despaired of life itself. Indeed, we felt that we had received the sentence of death. But that was to make us rely not on ourselves but on God who raises the dead. (2 Corinthians 1:8–9 ESV)

During his ministry in the communities of Asia Minor (modern Turkey), Paul suffered great "affliction." The word used in the NKJV is *troubles*; the NIV reads *hardships*. Referring to his "affliction," Paul said: "We were utterly burdened beyond our strength that we even despaired of life itself." The exact nature of his hardships is not stated, but it probably involved some form of beating and imprisonment that was so severe that they were desperate for their lives. Then, in verse 9 he added that things had become so bad that "we felt we had received the sentence of death." First, this indicates that Paul suffered so greatly that he thought he was about to die for the cause of Christ—and yet he was willing to make any sacrifice, just so others might come to know Jesus. Secondly, it suggests an even greater truth. For the gospel to be proclaimed regardless the cost, Paul had to die to self.

> Indeed, we felt that we had received the sentence of death. But that was to make us rely not on ourselves but *on God* who raises the dead. He delivered us from such a deadly peril, and he will deliver us. *On him we have set our hope* that he will deliver us again. (2 Corinthians 1:8–10 ESV) [Italics added for emphasis.]

Paul and his associates suffered so much that they realized they could not rely on themselves but only "on God." As he came to realize he might die serving Christ, Paul's reliance on Jesus Christ grew. Suffering helped him learn to place his entire hope in God. Realizing what it cost him to follow his Lord, Paul came to trust everything to the Lord—even whether he lived or died. The same thought was also captured in his letter to the Philippians: "For to me, to live is Christ, and to die is gain" (Philippians 1:21).

As we consider the great sacrifice made by so many to proclaim the message of the gospel, we also must ask: Why do other people resist surrendering themselves to Christ? Part of the reason is that we rely too heavily on ourselves—our own abilities and our own ideals. Somehow, our pride in ourselves and our human abilities keep us from surrendering control of our lives to Jesus. In addition, from somewhere within us, we feel such an attachment to the world that we dread giving up even a small portion of it. It seems that we fear God will lead us in a direction we really do not want to go. The fact is, too often we simply don't trust God to know what is best for our lives.

A young lady stood talking to an evangelist about consecration—of giving herself wholly to God. She said, "I dare not give myself wholly to the Lord, for fear he will send me out to China as a missionary."

The evangelist said, "If some cold, snowy morning a little bird should come, half-frozen, pecking at your window, and it would let you take it in and feed it, thereby putting itself entirely in your power, what would you do? Would you grip it in your hand and crush it? Or would you give it shelter, warmth, food, and care?"

A new light came into the girl's eyes. She said, "Oh, now I see, I see. I can trust God!" Two years later she again met the evangelist and recalled to him the incident. She told of how she had finally abandoned herself to God—and then her face lit up with a smile, and she said, "And do you know where God is going to let me serve him?" And there was now a twinkle in her eye. "In China!"[178]

In the words of the hymn writer:

> Trust and obey for there's no other way
> to be happy in Jesus than to trust and obey."[179]

Counting the cost leads us to trust God. Such trust is essential, if we are to follow him. "Being a disciple is a costly business. It calls for deliberate serious thought. The mission fields of the world can tell stories of would-be missionaries who, once the glamour wore off and the stark realities became evident, packed up and went back home. John Mark almost became such a 'missionary'" (Acts 12:25–13:5, 13).[180]

Rather than allowing the price to negatively influence our involvement in God's work, when we count the cost, we admit our own inability to accomplish in our own power the task God has placed before us. We count the cost so we might understand our utter dependency upon God, and then we place our complete hope and trust in our heavenly Father no matter what comes our way. We trust him because God has promised to always be with us, and nothing is impossible for him.

Please understand. The reason the Father calls on us to do the impossible is never just for ourselves. We may think it is, but it's not. It is all about him. Just as with the resurrection of Lazarus, God does the impossible that we might believe in him and glorify him.[181] None of this relieves us of doing our part, but it reminds us that when God calls us to obedience, he wants us to trust him completely to provide every resource we need. Regardless of the circumstances, we are to depend upon him and not our own abilities. This is what a young shepherd boy named David did as he walked out on the plain between the Israelite and Philistine armies to face Goliath. He gave himself completely over to God, and God gave him an impossible victory.[182] This is what happened when Elijah obeyed God and the LORD God defeated the six hundred prophets of Baal on Mount Carmel.[183] God did the impossible when he routed and destroyed the combined armies of Ammon, Moab, and Mount Seir as King Jehoshaphat led the people of Judah to face their enemy on the battlefield, not with weapons of war but by joining their voices in a song of thanksgiving and praise to the LORD God, and trusted him to bring the victory.[184] This was the response of Mary and Joseph as they gave themselves to raising as their own a child born of the Holy Spirit despite the cultural reaction regarding Mary's pregnancy.[185] This is the stand that Peter and John also made before the Jewish Sanhedrin as they declared, "We cannot but speak the things which we have seen and heard … We must obey God rather than men" (Acts 4:19–20, 5:29). Time after time, we discover in God's Word how individuals, as they follow his commands, gave themselves completely to the LORD God and called upon him for the impossible—and God responded by doing only what he could do. What we cannot do, God can, regardless of the circumstances! Do you believe this?

At the International Youth Triennium in Bloomington, Indiana, in July 1980, Professor Bruce Riggins of McCormick Theological Seminary was sharing with thirty-eight hundred attendees that he had met a very dedicated Christian working in an amazing way with the underprivileged people in London, England. He wanted to know what inspired her Christian faith and action. She shared her story of how seeing another Christian's faith converted her. She was a Jew fleeing the German Gestapo in France during World War II. She knew she was close to being caught, and she wanted to give up. She came to the home of a French Huguenot. A widow lady came to that home to say that it was time to flee to a new place. This Jewish lady said, "It's no use; they will find me anyway. They are so close behind."

The Christian widow said, "Yes, they will find someone here, but it's time for you to leave. Go with these people to safety. I will take your identification and wait here."

The Jewish lady then understood the plan; the Gestapo would come and find this Christian widow and think she was the fleeing Jew.

As Professor Riggins listened to this story, the Christian lady of Jewish descent looked him in the eye and said, "I asked her why she was doing that, and the widow responded, 'It's the least I can do; Christ has already done that and more for me.'" The widow was caught and imprisoned in the Jewish lady's place, allowing time for her to escape. Within six months the Christian widow was dead in the concentration camp.

This Jewish lady never forgot that. She too became a follower of Jesus Christ and lived her life serving others. She met God through the greatest love a person can give—personal self-sacrifice. In faith, an authentic Christian lives his or her life serving others, saying, "That's the least I can do considering what great sacrifices Christ has already made for me."[186]

It always warms my heart to read of how Peter and John returned from the court of the Sanhedrin "rejoicing that they were counted worthy to be treated shamefully on behalf of the Name [of Jesus]." They were able to react this way because a few days earlier they had led the early church to pray for "all boldness" that they may freely speak his Word. They knew it was dangerous to proclaim Jesus in the temple, but "filled with the Holy Spirit" they continued to speak "the word of God boldly" (Acts 5:41; 4:29, 31). Are we as bold knowing what it might cost us?

Following Jesus Christ implies risking everything for him. There is a third reason given by Jesus as to why we "cannot be his disciples."

> In the same way, therefore, every one of you who does not renounce all his possessions cannot be my disciple. (Luke 14:33)

The key word in the Greek, *apotassetai* means to "give up."[187] Such a translation can be found in the New International, as well as the New American Standard. In the New King James Version it reads: "forsake." According to *The Expositor's Bible Commentary,* "When used of persons, the verb means to take leave of or say good-by to someone. When used of things, it means to give up or renounce."[188]

Nothing could be clearer. Discipleship is serious business. The Lord's requirements are never easy. If we are to follow him, we cannot be casual about our commitment to him. We are to "give up" everything and everyone for the cause of Christ. If we truly follow Jesus, we can never permit our fears to control our decisions. We must never allow our possessions or anyone else to prevent us from doing his will. We cannot let public opinion influence our devotion to our Lord. We must never grant human wisdom the power to veto God's plan for our lives and churches. Finally, we must not tolerate anything in our personal lives that draws us away from our Master and Lord. Every sin in our lives, known and unknown, must be confessed before God and rooted out of our lives. We are to yield ourselves completely unto Jesus Christ. We are to become so committed to him "that we become spiritually and mentally free from worldly-mindedness, frivolity, covetousness, and selfishness. Then we are free to serve him without reservation."[189]

I realize we do all this at great personal peril. Our family may disown us. Our friends may desert us. Society will condemn, persecute, and even kill us. The organized church may even decry our efforts as it condemns and abandons us. But like the early followers of Christ, when we answer the call to follow Jesus, we risk everything by surrendering ourselves completely to him, and nothing else matters except proclaiming Jesus Christ, and him crucified.

There is one last word of caution that needs to be considered. **Failure to live for Christ may make us worthless to Christ.** Notice the Lord's final warning.

> Now, salt is good, but if salt should lose its taste, how will it be made salty? It isn't fit for the soil or for the manure pile; they throw it out. Let anyone who has ears to hear listen. (Luke 14:34–35)

In the simplest of terms, salt is noticed in food because it adds flavor to the food. But once salt has lost its taste, its influence upon our food is gone, and it cannot be made salty again. In which case, it isn't even worth being spread on the road to keep the weeds from growing! Instead, it is just thrown into the trash heap.

This brings before us a stunning truth for Christians. If we are "the salt of the earth" (Matthew 5:13)—if we are to influence the world for Jesus, we must commit ourselves fully unto him. There cannot be any half-hearted committed. There cannot be any compromise with the world. We cannot be double-minded in our commitment to the Master. Instead we are to give our very best to the Lord. Any failure on our part may mean we have become worthless and bound "for the manure pile." Yes, these are harsh words that warn of judgement, but they are totally in line with the Lord's call for complete devotion unto him.

In his devotional study of these words, William Barclay tells this story. "Once someone was talking to a great scholar about a younger man. He said, "So and so tells me that he was one of your students." The teacher answered devastatingly, "He may have attended my lectures, but he was not one of my students."[190] It is my prayer that the Most High Teacher would never have reason to say that you are not one of his disciples.

My brothers and sisters, if you are troubled by this idea, may you never forget that as long as one has breath, hope can still be found in the LORD. Only complete repentance and confession before God Almighty can save the one who has been declared worthless. Only by the power of the loving Creator of heaven and earth can all our sin be forgiven. Only through his sinless Son Jesus Christ are we restored unto his eternal presence. Only by the presence of his Spirit can we once again experience his boundless grace and infinite love.

It is an eternal truth that nothing is impossible for the LORD Jehovah. When we fail and yield to sin's temptation, and being human we will, only the omnipotent God can restore and make worthy once again the one he has declared unworthy. But we must come humbly before him seeking forgiveness and restoration. All praise to God, the Lord of lords and King of kings for he stands ready to forgive all our sin and renew our relationship with him.

"Let anyone who has ears to hear listen."

With these words by our Lord, we once again return to our theme—Jesus must be given first place in our lives. Following Jesus involves hating those we love, carrying our cross, and risking everything for Jesus. To do otherwise is to attempt to serve two masters—God and mammon[191]—and according to Jesus such a commitment is no commitment at all. We are to say, "Lord, all I have is yours."

Though skeptical of his teenage son's newfound determination to build bulging muscles, one father followed his teenager to the store's weight-lifting department, where they admired a set of weights.

"Please, Dad," pleaded the teen. "I promise I'll use 'em every day."

"I don't know, Michael. It's really a commitment on your part," the father said.

"Please, Dad?"

"They're not cheap either," the father said.

"I'll use 'em, Dad, I promise. You'll see."

Finally won over, the father paid for the equipment and headed for the door. After a few steps, he heard his son behind him say, "What! You mean I have to carry them to the car?"[192]

Isn't that how many of us are? We are committed until we are required to make an effort beyond what we are willing to give, and then we turn our backs on Jesus. We are willing to follow Jesus until the cost becomes too great, then we refuse to give any more of ourselves. We refuse to make any more sacrifices. My friend, are you following him with all your being? As you reconsider your relationship with the Lord, have you committed everything to him?

Food for Thought

What has it cost you to follow Jesus?

What price have you paid in you daily walk with Jesus?

Do you know an individual who has paid dearly for following Jesus? Have you read stories of such individuals? What did you learn from their account of their suffering for the cause of Jesus?

What did it cost Jesus to save you?

Once again, what has it cost you to follow Jesus?

Jesus looked around and said to his disciples, "How hard it is for those who have wealth to enter the kingdom of God!?" The disciples were astonished at his words.

Again, Jesus said to them, "Children, how hard it is to enter the kingdom of God! It is easier for a camel to go through the eye of a needle than for a rich person to enter the kingdom of God." They were even more astonished, saying to one another, "Then who can be saved??"

Looking at them, Jesus said, "With man it is impossible, but not with God, because all things are possible with God."

Peter began to tell him, "Look, we have left everything and followed you."

"Truly I tell you," Jesus said, "there is no one who has left house or brothers or sisters or mother or father or children or fields for my sake and for the sake of the gospel, who will not receive a hundred times more, now at this time—houses, brothers and sisters, mothers and children, and fields, with persecutions—and eternal life in the age to come. But many who are first will be last, and the last first." (Mark 10:23–31)

CHAPTER 5

The Call to Obedience

The title of a story filed by Jim Sandell in the Associated Press on September 15, 2004, reads as follows: "Student Collects Fake Parking Fines." According to the story:

A Wisconsin fraternity member has been arrested for using a unique method of supplementing his income, handing out fake parking tickets. Authorities say twenty-three-year-old Anthony Gallagher allegedly earned several hundred dollars by putting phony parking tickets on cars and having the duped owners send him the payment.

Investigators uncovered the scam in March 2003 when a victim tried to mail in a payment for a ticket but had it returned as undeliverable. Authorities say the trail led to Gallagher when they noticed the ticket was an exact copy of a parking ticket Gallagher had received in February 2003. The citation number on the phony tickets was the same number as on Gallagher's ticket.

Gallagher admitted that he had placed several of the phony tickets on vehicles parked near his fraternity. Authorities claim the young man set up a post office box and asked recipients to mail $40 tickets. He then placed the money, which amounted to several hundred dollars, in his personal bank account.[193]

More than two centuries ago, Paul warned another young man named Timothy, "The love of money is a root of all kinds of evil. Some people, eager for money have wandered away from the faith and pierced themselves with many griefs" (1 Timothy 6:10 NIV).

The Impossible Made Possible

Our story begins with young man who also had money trouble.[194] As Jesus was about to continue his journey down the east side of the Jordan toward Jerusalem,[195] a rich young man rushed up to him throwing respectability aside, knelt, and asked a question. "Good teacher, what shall I do to inherit eternal life?" The Lord's response was like a douse of cold water—"Why do you call me good? No one is good except God alone." In essence, he was saying, "What are you saying? Don't you know that by calling me good you are calling me God?"[196] From there, the Lord's unexpected reply left him with only two choices—either ignore the teacher's command or obey him as God.

One of the things we often fail to mention is that **following Jesus means obeying Jesus.** In answer to the young man's question, the Lord listed several of the commandments. I can imagine the pride that welled up in the young man as he said under his breath, "Yes! I've got this! This is easy." And then to Jesus, "I have kept all these all my life." As with many Jewish boys, he had very likely been trained from his youth the requirements of the law of Moses; therefore, mentally he understood the actions God demanded from his people, but not in his heart. Something else was in control there. It is very plausible that outwardly he had indeed kept these commands, but pride is a hard master. It can keep us from seeing the true nature of our faults. Even more, it can direct us to compare ourselves to those individuals with whom we stack up quite well. But following Jesus is more than checking off the boxes so we can boast of our accomplishments. It is more than 'looking good' when we compare ourselves to other people. Or excusing our halfway efforts at keeping his commands—just as long as we are better than the next guy. Following Jesus is recognizing him as the Son of the Most High and comparing ourselves to his perfect holiness—and coming up short and seeing our utter helplessness before him. It involves paying attention to his commands with all our heart, mind, strength and soul—and obeying him.

Also notice that even though "Jesus loved him," he did not pull his punches. He spoke the truth in love. It seems to me that the Lord was almost saying, "Yes, my son, you have lived according to the Ten Commands as much as humanly possible, but that's not good enough. There is something else more important you must do to be perfect. Go, sell all you have and give to the poor, and you will have treasure in heaven. Then come (take up your cross and) follow me.'" Regarding this statement, David Platt made this comment: "It's as if Jesus is saying to him, 'Give what you have to the poor; I'll give you something better.' In the end, Jesus is not calling this man away from treasure; he's calling him to treasure."[197]

This command of the Lord Jesus Christ is not implied; rather, it is very clear. Following Jesus is obeying him to the best of our ability. True discipleship is a willingness to give up everything and submit ourselves in total obedience unto the Son of God. As my reading has brought to my attention, if our children ignore our instructions, we would be concerned about their disobedience. We may even choose to discipline them for their disobedience and rebellion. For instance, we love them, but we simply cannot allow them to play in a busy highway because they would get hurt. The LORD God is equally concerned about our disobedience—and his concerns are even more important because they are about eternal life or death. As his children, when we refuse to obey him, we are not following him, despite any reasoning to the opposite. Disobedience, even in the slightest way, is still being rebellious and sinful toward God. As Dietrich Bonhoeffer reminds us in *The Cost of Discipleship*, "The life of discipleship is ... obedience to the Son of God."[198]

Instead of following Jesus, we are told this young rich man "went away grieving, because he had many possessions." To following Jesus required him to make a greater sacrifice than he was willing to make. He was called to obey Jesus, but his possessions were more important than following Jesus. They were more important than eternal life. Remember he came asking, "What must I do to inherit eternal life?" Simply stated, he was unwilling to obey Jesus—except on his own terms. I find it interesting that "only here in the gospels is a command of Jesus to follow him clearly rejected,"[199] although we know others also refused to follow Jesus.

As I think about the young man's decision, I find myself wondering: Have I made the same decision? Have I allowed my wealth, or my desire for more wealth, to keep me from surrendering to the Lord? What about you? Has your wealth or lack of wealth kept you from truly following Jesus? How many times have we said, "Lord, I'll follow you if ..." If you will allow me to live like my friends and do what they do. I will follow you if you will bless me with wealth, popularity, and position. I will follow if you do not demand that I give up certain things in my life. My friend, we have the same choice this young man had. There are only two choices, not the four or five we would like. We can follow Jesus on his terms, or we can choose to follow our own desires and be disobedient unto him. No compromise is available. In our society, as with this young rich man, perhaps the hardest things to leave behind are our possessions.

Out of his eternal love, Jesus wanted this young ruler as a disciple, yet the young man went away rejecting him. Never one to miss a teachable moment, the Lord watched him leave and sadly commented to his disciples,

> How hard it is for those who have wealth to enter
> the kingdom of God!? (Mark 10:23)

According to Jesus, **it is almost impossible for rich people to be saved.** No one wants to hear this. So why is this so difficult, even impossible?[200] The answer is very simple. As the young rich man showed, it is our wealth as well as all that wealth promises—the possessions, the popularity, the prestige, and the power—that often motivates us to turn our backs on Jesus. The rich young man rejected Jesus when he was asked to give his wealth away—and then follow Jesus. He wanted to follow Jesus on his own terms.

We see a similar reaction in the parable of the sower as individuals allow "the cares of this world and the deceitfulness of riches choke the word, and [they] becomes unfruitful" (Matthew 13:22 NKJV). The individual's wealth or desire for more wealth prevented the word of Jesus Christ from bearing fruit in his life. In addition, under the influence of the world we have reached the wrong conclusion that great wealth is a sign of God's blessing, and hardship is a sign of God's disapproval. Either can be, but this is not the complete truth. Some believers in both the New and Old Testaments had great wealth, but there are those who also lived in poverty. Regardless of what the prosperity theology may proclaim, wealth is not always a sign of God's blessing. This was the opinion of the friends of Job: "The wicked man will not be rich" (Job 15:29).[201] No wonder the disciples were amazed at the Lord's teaching.

Can the same thing be said about us? It really does not matter whether we have a lot of possessions or just a few with hopes for more, somehow without even realizing what is happening, what we possess comes to possess us. Somewhere along the way, we have developed a love-affair with our money, and in the process our things—our stuff, our possessions—have become more important than our relationship with God. In this regard, Warren W. Wiersbe warns, "Money is a marvelous servant but a terrible master. If you possess money, be grateful and use it for God's glory; but if money possesses you, beware!"[202] It is so easy to allow our wealth to become the center of our lives, and before long, we turn our focus to protecting our wealth and accumulating even more wealth. When this happens, we ignore Christ and the part he should play in our lives.

Before you become defensive, let me remind you that we live in the wealthiest nation in the world. For the most part, the poorest person in the good old USA is wealthier than most of the people around the world. In my brief travels, I have seen people in Sao Paulo, Brazil, who had nothing, living in boxes in the middle of a four-lane highway. Perhaps you have seen as I have the news stories from Africa, Southeast Asia, and other places where men and women, boys and girls, old and young alike are starving to death because of war, disease, and famine. For this reason, I would suggest the high probability that millions of people in the world live on far less than we waste. Even in our nation, if we can believe a billboard I recently observed, one in six children in our nation goes to bed hungry every night. That is a bitter pill to accept in the middle of so much wealth. And to think, we complain when our meal is occasionally late; we become upset if it is not cooked as we might like it.

I have become even more aware of the huge part wealth plays in our lives during my mission trips to Armenia. Going there, we carry two suitcases stuffed full of personal items, teaching supplies, and medical supplies. As we pack to returned home, we place everything in one suitcase. Most of our sheets, towels, and clothing items—shirts, pants, and shoes, etc.—are placed in a designated area for the Armenians for two reasons. The first reason is so we would not be charged by the airlines for a half-full suitcase on the way home. But what I want you to hear is this. We give these items to the Armenians who desperately need them. Even a ziplock bag is treasured and reused by the Armenians.

This was made even more real to me when one year my wife left behind a pair of shoes (which, by the way, were well worn). Two years later when I returned, one of our translators was proudly wearing those shoes. And she was still wearing them the next year. This made me realize that most of the world is so very poor, and I mean poor, especially when placed beside all the things that we have accumulated. Yet they are so grateful for the little they have, while we are so ungrateful for our sizable bounty.

I say this not to proclaim a social gospel, but to help you

understand that wealth does not keep us from God's kingdom, but our love for it does. Like the rich young ruler, our riches—our wealth, our possessions—can come between us and our commitment to Jesus. As our riches increase, Jesus slips in our lives to a place of lesser importance. For this reason, whether we like it or not, in America and probably other places as well, it is extremely difficult, if not impossible, for rich people to be saved because of our attachment to our wealth.

Writing to Timothy, the apostle Paul addressed this issue, saying, "Command those who are rich in the present world not to be arrogant nor to put their hope in wealth, but to put their hope in God, who richly provides us with everything for our enjoyment" (1 Timothy 6:17 NIV). This applies to every individual who claims to follow Jesus. Rather than focusing on acquiring earthly riches, we must learn to "set our hope on God." Let us not forget that our Lord expressed the same idea first in the Sermon on the Mount.

> Don't store up for yourselves treasures on earth, where moth and rust destroy and where thieves break in and steal. But store up for yourselves treasures in heaven, where neither moth nor rust destroys, and where thieves don't break in and steal. For where your treasure is, there your heart will be also. ... No one can serve two masters, since either he will hate one and love the other, or he will be devoted to one and despise the other. You cannot serve both God and money. (Matthew 6:19–21, 24)

In the next verse Jesus made money even more of a hindrance to salvation: "It is easier for a camel to go through the eye of a needle than for a rich man to enter the kingdom of God" (Mark 10:25 KJV). According to most commentators, we should take this colorful statement literally. It is literally physically impossible for a camel to go through the eye of a needle. In our materialism, we seek loopholes and shortcuts to salvation, while Jesus offers us none. Some have even come to feel our wealth entitles us to God's good grace. In doing so, they fail to see that the Lord was emphasizing the truth that "those who are ruled by money cannot be ruled by God."[203] Overwhelmed to the point of being dumbfounded,[204] the disciples asked, "Who then can be saved?" (Mark 10:26 KJV).

Please understand this: **God can save anyone**—even the wealthiest among us or the most sin-hardened individual. He can even save *you*! Although he appeared to ignore the young man's request regarding eternal life, Jesus answered the disciples:

> With man it is impossible, but not with God, because all things are possible with God. (Mark 10:27)

The phrase "it is impossible" shuts the door and seals it to man's ability to save himself.[205] The simple truth is that it is God who saves man; try as he might, man cannot save himself. We cannot save ourselves through our good works. We cannot save ourselves by being good, moral people or by seeking to live according to the Sermon on the Mount. As with the young man, eternal life cannot be earned by obeying the Ten Commandments or even the whole Bible. If this were true, the Pharisees and other Jewish religious leaders were saved by their actions. The Bible makes it clear that we are saved only by faith in Jesus, the Son of the Living God, who gave himself for us on the cross of Calvary.

Think back with me more than two thousand years to the day Jesus was crucified. In Luke's account of the crucifixion,[206] hanging on each side of our Lord was a thief—one hung to his right and the other to his left. To my knowledge, no one has ever questioned whether these men deserved their punishment. After all, they were known thieves. As that horrible day progressed, one thief in his anguish joined the mob gathered at the foot of their crosses in mocking Jesus and calling upon him to save himself—and them from their respective crosses. But at some point the other thief apparently realized Jesus was different and rebuked his comrade in thievery. He acknowledged their guilt while declaring Jesus's innocence. Then he simply said, "Lord, remember me when You come into Your kingdom." Ignoring the unrepentant thief, Jesus replied to him, "Assuredly I say to you, today you will be with Me in paradise" (Luke 23:42–43 NKJV).

Jesus responded by saving this one who made a simple request, even though he was a known thief and would die a thief. Judging from the company the two apparently kept—a man named Barnabas—they may have been revolutionaries who had stolen and murdered in the name of revolution against Rome. Definitely not the type of men we would think should be saved, but Jesus saved the one who called on him.

As difficult as it may be to comprehend, if they had honestly asked in godly repentance, Jesus would have saved the religious leaders who hated him so much that they had planned for months to kill him.[207] Then they had physically abused him all night before bringing him to Pilate to be crucified. Through the grace of God, the same is true of all the other people gathered at Calvary. Our Lord would have saved any person from the crowd that mocked and ridiculed him. The same is true of the soldiers that nailed his hands and feet to the cross and gambled at his feet for his clothing. If Pilate or Herod had come in utter repentance and made such a request, Jesus would have saved either one of them. Even Judas, who betrayed him with a kiss, could have been forgiven and saved if he had come to Jesus in repentance and faith. All that was necessary was for the individual to come to him by faith, confessing and repenting his sin. The simple fact is that Jesus can save even the worst person who has ever walked upon the world—if he or she would but come to him in repentance and faith. No evil deed is too great to prevent our salvation, if by faith we come to Jesus. Such is the greatness of God's love for humankind. Salvation does not remove the consequences of our sin here on earth, but with God, eternal salvation is possible for anyone through the shed blood of Jesus Christ.

So how does the impossible become possible? It occurs when we are born again by the power of the Holy Spirit. Jesus summed it up with these words to Nicodemus: "For God so loved the world that he gave his only begotten Son, that whoever believes in him should not perish but have everlasting life" (John 3:16 NKJV).

Salvation can be ours because God in his boundless love chose to send Jesus, his only begotten Son, from heaven to earth to die in our place. Jesus, who never committed a single sin in his entire life, became a perfect, sinless sacrifice who freely gave of his life that we might live.[208] In his mercy, God chose not to condemn us because of our sin but to lay our sin upon his own Son, Jesus Christ. It was Jesus who suffered and died on the cross to pay the full penalty for our sin. Before sin even entered this world, in his grace, an all-knowing God chose to offer us something we do not deserve—the gift of salvation. Jesus died on the cross so that whosoever believes in him may have the right to be called a son of God.[209]

Please understand this. We do not in any way deserve salvation. There is nothing we can do to earn the privilege of being God's children. There is not enough money on the entire planet to buy our way into God's eternal kingdom. There is no sacrifice we can make that will gain us eternal life. It all depends upon our willingness to believe in Jesus Christ as the one and only Son of God. In his letter to the Ephesians, Paul declared,

> For you are saved by grace through faith, and *this is not from yourselves*; it is God's gift —not from works, so that no one can boast. (Ephesians 2:8–9) [Italics added for emphasis.]

Salvation is the gift of God, which is awarded to the person who comes by faith to Jesus Christ, who gave his life that we might live. Jesus is the Savior who came to seek and save the lost and sinful people of the world. He is the Lord of heaven and earth who conquered death by arising from the dead on the third day. Jesus is the coming King of kings and Lord of lords who is waiting until the right instant in time to return and claim his kingdom and his people. At this very moment, he is sitting at the right hand of God the Father interceding for those who come by faith to him.[210] Based upon his sacrifice on Calvary, Jesus is our righteous advocate before the heavenly Father declaring our innocence based on our faith in him. And he rejoices with his angels every time one lost sinner comes confessing his or her sin and turns from that sin unto him.[211]

My friend, please hear me clearly when I say that only Jesus can save you! Do you know my Savior and Lord? If not, will you believe in Jesus right now? Will you come to him by faith in his sacrifice on the cross of Calvary?

Jesus said on one occasion as he invited the children into his arms: "Truly, I say to you, whoever does not receive the kingdom of God like a child shall not enter it" (Mark 10:15 ESV). There is a certain innocence about children. It is not unusual for them to believe without any real reason to believe. They are not too arrogant and proud to believe. They tend to accept things without all the questions and competing angles that disturb and drive away adults. Will you, with the same simple faith as a child, come to Jesus? Will you in this moment listen to the call of the Savior and open yourself up to the presence of Jesus?

The Blessings of the Lord

As I think about the sacrifice Jesus made on the cross, my thoughts turn to the day when I found him as my Savior and Lord. He had always been reaching out to me; but I had been running from him since the seventh grade. I was fifteen at the time. It was a Sunday afternoon, and a teenager younger than I came by the house to talk with me about Jesus. Although I listened, I did not immediately respond. Like so many times before, I tried to put the decision off until later, but something was different this time. Jesus was calling, and his Spirit would not let me go. As this one who would become a friend left, I could not escape the Spirit's loving pull. Its presence lingered on, speaking so gently to my troubled heart. So much so, that evening during the worship service when I could no longer ignore him, I surrendered to his call. Walking down the aisle, I took the pastor's hand announcing my decision to the church. What a joy entered my heart and sweep through my life. The joy of the Lord has been with me ever since. Yes, there have been trying times, and temptation has often led to sin, but the Spirit's presence has always restored his joy to my heart and soul as I sought my Savior anew in repentance and confession. And as I have sought to walk with him down through the years, the blessings from the Lord have been beyond imagination.

Please understand that **those who come by faith to Jesus will be blessed on earth.** As it dawned on Peter that they had done exactly what Jesus demanded of the young man, he exclaimed, "See, we have left everything and followed you." In Matthew's Gospel, we find these additional words: "So what will there be for us?" (Matthew 19:27). Like we often do, Peter appeared to be saying: "What will we get out of following you?"

Apparently cutting Peter's comment off, Jesus answered with a promise.

> Truly I tell you, ... there is no one who has left house or brothers or sisters or mother or father or children or fields for my sake and for the sake of the gospel, who will not receive a hundred times more, now at this time—houses, brothers and sisters, mothers and children, and fields, with persecutions—and eternal life in the age to come. (Mark 10:29–30)

With these words, Jesus promised that if we follow him completely, we will receive blessings far better—a hundred times better than anything we could ever hope to receive without Christ. Yes, some will be physical blessings upon this earth. But most rewards will be of a spiritual nature that the nonbeliever can never understand because he has no part in Christ. Among the blessings Jesus listed for those individuals who forsake everything to follow him are the physical blessings of houses and farms, and all that comes with them. In addition, we will become a part of a whole new family, which will be both physical and spiritual in nature, as we are born by faith into the family of God. Earlier the Lord had said, "looking at those sitting in a circle around him, 'Here are my mother and my brothers! Whoever does the will of God is my brother and sister and mother'" (Mark 3:34–35 NIV). Through Christ we have new family. If you are saved, as followers of Jesus, you are my spiritual brother and sister in Christ. We have an extended family far beyond anything we could ever imagine. It extends forth and backward through time, going around the world to include all those who have been faithful to God. Doesn't this sound great? But don't stop there. Look a little further. Jesus added another interesting but troubling phrase: "with persecutions."

Not only does following Jesus bring spiritual and physical blessing, but **also obedience may lead to great trial and trouble.** This is also something we don't want to think about, but the Lord would later further affirm this by saying: "Remember the word I said to you: 'A servant is not greater than his master.' If they persecuted me, they will also persecute you ... They will make you outcasts from the synagogues, but an hour is coming for everyone who kills you to think he is offering service to God" (John 15:20; 16:2 NASB). Returning to this theme later in the evening, Jesus lovingly said, "All this I have told you so that you will not fall away ... In this world you will have trouble" (John 16:1, 33 NIV). In other words, Jesus warned that persecution was coming so the believer might remain faithful when it came upon him or her. Paul also cautioned Timothy that "everyone who wants to live a godly life in Christ Jesus will be persecuted" (2 Timothy 3:12 NIV). The fact is, according to scripture, some form of persecution is a forgone conclusion for the child of God. To the Philippians, Paul said, "For it has been granted to you on behalf of Christ not only to believe in him, but also to suffer for him" (Philippians 1:29 NIV).

I can almost hear someone shouting, "*What?* Why are you really talking about suffering? I signed up for all the blessings, but I didn't sign up to be persecuted." This is the reaction that has led us to completely misinterpret the idea of blessings. We have come to expect only good blessing from God. For this reason, when we encounter persecution, we find ourselves saying, "What have I done to deserve this?" According to the Bible, if we follow Jesus in this world, we will experience the blessing of being persecuted for our Lord. We will suffer for his sake. Stated another way, "since we are his children, we are his heirs. In fact, together with Christ we are heirs of God's glory. But if we are to share his glory, we must also share his suffering" (Romans 8:17 NLT). Our heavenly Father has not only called us to believe in Jesus, but he has blessed us with the privilege of suffering for Jesus Christ. Jesus declared in the Beatitudes:

> Blessed are those who are persecuted for righteousness' sake, For theirs is the kingdom of heaven. Blessed are you when they revile and persecute you, and say all kinds of evil against you falsely for My sake. Rejoice and be exceedingly glad, for great is your reward in heaven, for so they persecuted the prophets who were before you. (Matthew 5:9–12 NKJV)

In the early days of the church, the disciples took these words to heart as they rejoiced "that they had been considered worthy to suffer shame for his name." According to Luke's history of the early church in the book of Acts, in one instance Peter and John were "flogged [by the Sanhedrin] ... and ordered ... not to speak in the name of Jesus," but their suffering only drew them closer to the Lord, which in turn encouraged them to be even bolder as they proclaimed the gospel "in the temple and from house to house" (Acts 5:40–42 NASB). I am always amazed to read the stories in Acts of Paul's missionary journeys. On several occasions he was beaten and at least once left for died, but he got back up and faithfully continued his journey to another city to proclaim Jesus Christ, and him crucified. I rejoice as I can almost hear him singing hymns of praise at midnight from the innermost part of the jail in Philippi—after being unjustly beaten with rods.[212] In 2 Corinthians 11:23–33, Paul shared some of his troubles and tribulation in order to encourage the church during its time of persecution. James, the brother of Jesus, encouraged the church saying, "Consider it all joy, my brothers and sisters, when you experience various trials" (James 1:2 NASB). Speaking to the church, Peter wrote, "Household slaves, submit to your master ... when you do what is good and suffer, if you endure it, this brings favor with God. For you were called to this, because Christ also suffered for you, leaving you an example, that you should follow in his steps" (1 Peter 2:18–21). Then he added in the next chapter: "But even if you should suffer for the sake of righteousness, you are blessed. ... For it is better, if God should will it so, that you suffer for doing good than for doing wrong" (1 Peter 3:14, 17 NASB).

The sheer number of references to suffering and persecution makes it abundantly clear that for the New Testament church, persecution was the natural result of obedience. But this begs the question for the modern believer: Are we truly being obedient to the Lord, if we are not suffering for the sake of the gospel? And perhaps even more importantly: Has our freedom from persecution made it too easy to compromise the truths of the gospel? My reading about Christian persecution around the world seems to indicate that when the church is under extreme hardship, people grow in their relationship to Jesus Christ. Is it possible that churches in North America are not growing because our lives have become too easy?

Think about it for a moment. Are you as close to the Lord as you should be? Why not?

Regardless of what you may have heard, suffering is a normal part of following Jesus Christ. "The pressure of persecution did not mean that God wasn't keeping his promises or that the disciples had been wrong in putting faith in him. Rather, during persecution, God still blesses all those who believe in him."[213] In fact, reading the gospel accounts almost seems to indicate that persecuted believers are blessed far beyond those of us who endure little, if any, oppression.

So how can suffering and persecution be considered a blessing, you may ask? Since such a discussion is not our purpose at this time, please allow to me to suggest just three of the many blessings that come from persecution.

First, suffering is a blessing because it draws us closer to God. The lives of the early followers are prime examples of this. They walked every day in the power of the Holy Spirit. In 2 Corinthians, Paul mentioned that he was suffering from a thorn in the flesh. The exact nature of the thorn is unknown, but God refused to remove the thorn and answered his prayers, saying, "My grace is sufficient for you, for my strength is made perfect in weakness." In essence God said to Paul, "I have given you 'My grace' and 'My strength.' 'My presence' is all you need." Blessed by the indwelling presence of the Holy Spirit, Paul was able to say, "Most gladly I will rather boast in my infirmities, that the power of Christ may rest upon me." Through the "power of Christ," Paul was drawn the closest to God during the moments of his greatest suffering. When he felt he was unable to continue, the apostle was pulled so close to God that he was able to say, "When I am weak, then I am strong" (2 Corinthians 12:7–10). Even when suffering physical pain and mental anguish, Paul could say, "The life I now live in the flesh, I live by faith in the Son of God, who loved me and gave himself for me" (Galatians 2:20 KJV).

Second, God uses our suffering to provide a godly example to others. How we react to the heartache, pain, and loss of life is an example of what God can do when we rely on him as we endue personal tribulation. God uses the Christlike character we demonstrate in the middle of what may be unfair persecution to influence both the saved and the unsaved for Christ. Our suffering encourages other people in the middle of their pain. It can even draw the unsaved to Christ. Paul explained it this way to the Thessalonians.

> And you became imitators of us and of the Lord, for you received the word in much affliction, with the joy of the Holy Spirit, so that you *became an example* to all the believers in Macedonia and in Achaia. (1 Thessalonians 1:6–7, ESV) [Italics added for emphasis.]

Third, our suffering and trials prepare us to encourage and help those individuals who are going through equally difficult times in their lives. In the opening chapter of 2 Corinthians we read:

> Blessed be the God and Father of our Lord Jesus Christ, the Father of mercies and the God of all comfort, who comforts us in all our affliction so that we will be able to comfort those who are in any affliction with the comfort we ourselves are comforted by God. (2 Corinthians 1:3–4 NASB)

We can comfort other people in their sorrow and suffering because we too have experienced the same thing and understand— at least in part—what they are going through. In our pain and suffering we received comfort "from God"—through the presence of the Comforter, the Holy Spirit. This enables us to walk up to that one who is hurting, throw our arms around him or her, and with tears in our eyes say, "I understand"—and they are encouraged because they know we really do understand their pain. By this simple act of support, we "rejoice with those who rejoice, and weep with those who weep" and we become "of the same mind toward one another" in Christ Jesus (Romans 12:15–16 NASB).

As a pastor I have seen this played out in the church as individuals opened their lives and shared their pain and suffering with not necessarily the whole church—that could be too overwhelming—but with a few chosen individuals. The mutual ministry of godly love blessed not only them but also those who become involved in their lives as they cared for one another in Christ Jesus. Such sacrificial love also flowed over and blessed the entire church body in unbelievable ways. I will always remember the faces and names of those hurting souls who invited me into their troubled lives, and the blessing they engraved on my life. But I have also witnessed those individuals who like lone rangers closed the door to others to keep their difficulties—their pain—private. I would suggest that they often miss so many of the blessings God wanted to bestow upon them during the most difficult times of life. This is one of the real tragedies of our faith—people who believe the lie of the devil that our faith is a private matter not to be shared with anyone—even with close friends and family. I have come to believe that suffering is one of the greatest opportunities used by God to help believers grow in Christian love and fellowship. As children of God, our lives were meant to be open books so others can see and experience our faith and glorify the heavenly Father—especially during tragic circumstances.

My Christian brothers and sister, in your troubles please do not lose sight of the fact that suffering and persecution serve a purpose in our lives. According to Peter, "You suffer grief in various trials so that the proven character of your faith … may result in praise, glory and honor at the revelation of Jesus Christ" (1 Peter 1:6–7). While we are going through our personal tribulation, it is often difficult to see how this is possible, but somehow in the mysteries of God, he uses everything that happens in the lives of his children, whether good or bad, for his glorify and his purpose. Many times we can only see him at work with hindsight, and at other times we may not discover his divine purpose until we see him face to face. Regardless of our circumstances, we strive to faithfully obey him. As one commentator has suggested: "Don't dwell on what you have given up; think about what you have gained, and give thanks for it. You can never out give God."[214]

Let us never forget Paul's words of encouragement to the church in Rome during her time of persecution.

> We rejoice in our sufferings, knowing that suffering produces endurance, endurance produces character, and character produces hope, and hope does not put us to shame, because God's love has been poured into our hearts through the Holy Spirit who has been given to us. (Romans 5:3–5 ESV)

In addition, **those who obey Jesus will be rewarded in heaven.** One writer made this comment: "Sacrifice is required if you would gain heavenly reward. The disciples paid a high price. They may not have given up as much as the rich man would have had to give up; but it is not how much you give up, but how much is left that gives us the extent of your sacrifice."[215]

When we consider the future, there are several things about rewards that become evident. First, all earthly blessings are from God, but most are also temporal; they will not last. Even persecution and suffering, no matter how harsh, will come to an end. In addition, Jesus suggested in the Sermon on the Mount that physical blessing and rewards can be lost—they might be eaten by moths, destroyed by rust, or stolen by thieves. On the other hand, spiritual rewards from God are eternal. No one can take them away from us because their source is God. Besides, most of our rewards are stored in the vaults of heaven, and only the heavenly Father holds the keys. For this reason, while on earth we are to seek to store up spiritual rewards in heaven, rather than physical rewards on earth.[216] By faith, the ultimate reward of eternal life in God's presence is awarded to the one who faithfully follows Jesus.

Second, lest we forget, "we will live with him by God's power" (2 Corinthians 13:4). Our lives are pleasing to our Lord because we are the temple of the Holy Spirit and his indwelling power.[217] It is his Spirit that enables us to "walk worthy of the Lord, fully pleasing to him: bearing fruit in every good work, and growing in the knowledge of God" (Colossians 1:10). It is the indwelling presence of the Holy Spirit that empowers us to face the difficulties of life. This is important because how we live on earth is our greatest proof of how much we love the Lord Jesus Christ.

Third, while we "wait" on this earth for Christ's return,[218] we are to live lives "pleasing to him" because we love him. And when Christ returns, our heavenly rewards will be given us "so that each of us may receive what is due us for the things done while in the body, whether good or bad" (2 Corinthians 5:8–10, Revelation 22:12 NIV). With this same thought in mind, the apostle John warned, "Watch yourselves, that you do not lose what we have accomplished, but that you may receive a full reward" (2 John 1:8 NASB).

Finally, regardless of what popular opinion may be, not everyone will be rewarded with a heavenly home. This is extremely difficult to accept. But remember, Jesus told us that "the gate is narrow and difficult is the way that leads to life, and … few will find it" (Matthew 7:14 NKJV). As awful and unloving as it may sound, we cannot ignore the fact that Jesus warned that everyone who enters by the wide gate and follows the broad road is headed to destruction. A few weeks later he stated that not everyone who cries to him, "Lord, Lord, will see the kingdom of heaven." Then he explained that it depends upon whether we choose to confess or deny him before men as to whether he will confess or deny us before his Father.[219] The truth is, it is not enough to say, "I'm a Christian." We must believe in Jesus and live like we believe in him.

So once again, what did Jesus say to his disciples? In Matthew's account of this story, we read that "everyone who has left houses or brothers or sisters or father or mother or children or fields because of my name will receive a hundred times more and will inherit eternal life" (Matthew 19:29). In other words, our heavenly Father is holding incredible rewards in heaven for each one of his children. But also understand this; we follow Jesus "for [his] name's sake"—not the rewards. Only those who humbly come to Jesus in repentance will receive his or her eternal rewards. Only those who come by faith in Jesus as the Son of God can be called his children of God.[220]

This is the great truth expressed by the missionary and martyr Jim Elliot: "He is no fool who gives what he cannot keep to gain what he cannot lose."[221]

Please allow me to make one final comment. **Only those individuals who humble themselves truly follow Jesus.** Our Lord expressed it this way several times in the gospels.[222] Look at verse 31 in Mark's gospel:

> But many who are first will be last, and the last first.
> (Mark 10:31)

Perhaps this was a rebuke to Peter regarding his "me-first" attitude. But it also is a warning against allowing our pride to control our lives.[223] At the same time, it speaks of a humility we do not often see. It suggests that those who refuse to humble themselves are focused upon themselves. Their thoughts are: "How might I get ahead in this world? What can I gain from serving Jesus? How can I get more of Christ's blessings?"

Although Jesus calls everyone, these are the people who are too wrapped up in themselves to follow Jesus. They are too prideful to submit to Jesus. They are too busy satisfying their own personal desires. Following Jesus means we are focused on him, and in turn, we recognize and acknowledge our willful, sinful nature before the LORD God of heaven and earth. Laying aside our pride, by the power of the Holy Spirit, we humble ourselves and turn from our sin to Jesus. Seeking to glorify our Lord, we strive every day toward holiness so we might become meek and mild like Jesus. It implies that we will become quick to forgive and slow to anger, while showing others the same love, grace, and mercy God has shown us.

When we humble and submit ourselves unto Christ, our focus turns from, "What can I get from Jesus?" to "How can I show my love for Jesus?" No sacrifice for God's kingdom is too great. No command from the Lord is too difficult to obey. Under the influence of the Spirit, we find ourselves with an inward desire to give and give again, although it may hurt deeply. Such sacrifice was witnessed by Jesus as a poor widow dropped everything she had into the temple offering.[224] We discover this type of love among the believers in Corinth as they give out of their "abundance of joy and their extreme poverty" to help their brothers in Jerusalem during a time of famine. Even though they had nothing themselves, "they gave according to their means … and beyond their means … begging us earnestly for the favor of taking part in the relief of the saints." According to Paul, "they gave themselves first to the Lord and then by the will of God to us" (2 Corinthians 8:2–5 ESV).

I personally experienced this as one Sunday morning a godly man in my church handed me a hundred-dollar bill, even though he had lost his job and had been unable to find work for several months. His words to me that morning were filled with joy from the Spirit: "God has told me to give this to you." Overwhelmed with the thought—how can he afford to do this?—I could only thank him and the Lord for his generous gift of love. Down through the years, his example has led me to open my heart and be more generous when helping others. I have come to understand that it was because he deeply loved the Lord that he really had no choice but to obey him. And I have come to realize that God blesses each of us so we might use that blessing to bless other people in his name.

When we humble ourselves, we give sacrificially to those in need.

Our obedience to his commands comes from a loving surrender to his Lordship. We are willing to follow our Lord's example and with the attitude of a servant wash the feet of other individuals.[225] We love our neighbor as Jesus loves him. Through the Spirit's influence we freely give ourselves, our talents, our time, and our money unto the King of kings and Lord of lords—without expecting anything in return. We are willing to make any sacrifice for the cause of Jesus Christ that others may come to know and love our Lord. Our thoughts turn from "what I want" to "how can I glorify him? How can I show his love to another person? How can I best serve, honor and glorify my Lord?" No sacrifice made in the name of Jesus Christ is too great.

A chance meeting at a retreat gave a Detroit woman something she had sought for years—a new kidney. Forty-nine-year-old Lorraine Lamb had been on dialysis for six years. Although all three of her children had been tested for compatibility for donating, none of them had been able to help their mother. Lamb had resigned herself to a life on dialysis, which cleaned her blood but left her exhausted and demoralized.

Glenda McCloskey came to the retreat to meet her sister, but her trip changed when she happened to meet Lamb and hear her story. McCloskey said, "I was just amazed at how different her life would be if she had a kidney, so I thought, 'I'll give her one.' It seemed a small thing to make a big difference in someone's life."

Tests confirmed that McCloskey was a match, so she went through with the procedure to give a kidney to Lamb. Afterward Lamb said, "It was kind and wonderful. What else would a Christian do, but I didn't think she understood the depths of what she was offering."

McCloskey's family was not concerned about her decision to help another. McCloskey said that her family was used to her little adventures. Afterward, McCloskey added, "This has all been very rewarding. There's no better feeling than knowing you can help someone else. That's what life's about."[226]

Jesus said to his disciples, "Greater love hath no man than this, that a man lay down his life for his friends" (John 15:13 KJV). There is no greater love we can express for our Lord Jesus Christ than to completely submit ourselves unto him as Lord of our lives or than to be willing to sacrifice everything for Jesus. Are you following Jesus with all your being? If not, what are you holding back? What is keeping you from yielding everything to Jesus?

Food for Thought

Have you ever been called to give up something very important to you for the sake of the cross? How did you respond? Why did you respond as you did?

Have you ever suffered for obeying Jesus? Think about the situation. What did you learn spiritually about your ordeal?

What does your obedience say about your relationship to the Lord Jesus Christ?

Now some Greeks were among those who went up to worship at the festival. So they came to Philip, who was from Bethsaida in Galilee, and requested of him, "Sir, we want to see Jesus."

Philip went and told Andrew; then Andrew and Philip went and told Jesus.

Jesus replied to them, "The hour has come for the Son of Man to be glorified. Truly I tell you, unless a grain of wheat falls to the ground and dies, it remains by itself. But if it dies, it produces much fruit.

The one who loves his life will lose it, and the one who hates his life in this world will keep it for eternal life.

If anyone serves me, he must follow me. Where I am, there my servant also will be. If anyone serves me, the Father will honor him. (John 12:20–26)

CHAPTER 6

The Call to Service

I recently was reminded that victorious sports teams are often invited to visit with the president after winning a championship. Of course, some choose not to go for any number of reasons, but most see it as an honor to visit the White House. During their visit they are usually fed some type of food, and photographs are taken with the president. A big deal is made of the visit, and it makes all the various news outlets. But just suppose I wanted to have an audience with the president of our great nation. I could make my request, but I would probably discover it was quiet a difficult matter to obtain such an invitation because I'm just an average guy. I am not listed among the wealthy of our nation. I have not won any big sporting event. I'm not a celebrity. I have not accomplished some great deed or made an important discovery. I would be just an average Joe who wanted to talk with the president and share my opinions about the country.

The Lord's Sacrifice

The event before us began with a group of ordinary Greeks who came seeking an audience with Jesus.[227] From all appearances they were in Jerusalem for the Passover feast; in which case, it is possible they were proselytes to the Jewish faith. In their search for meaning in life, they came to Philip saying, "Sir, we want to see Jesus." It seems they had heard all about this man called Jesus, and they came looking for him to find out for themselves if all they had heard was true.

Phillip, on the other hand, was one of the first to follow Jesus.[228] When he first met Jesus, he had sought his friend Nathaniel and brought him to Jesus.[229] During the years that followed, Phillip had most likely brought other people to Jesus, but somehow on this occasion it appears that Phillip was not sure what he should do. Why? We can only guess. He was certainly not a stranger to Gentiles; after all, Philip was a Greek name, and he came from Bethsaida, which is only ten miles from Phoenicia, a Gentile nation.[230] Perhaps, like most Jews, he held a sense of prejudice against all Gentiles. It is possible Philip was concerned about the reaction of the multitude if Jesus met with these Gentiles.[231] Maybe he remembered Jesus saying to a Gentile woman, "I was sent except to the lost sheep of the house of Israel" (Matthew 15:24 NKJV). Perhaps he believed it was his duty to protect Jesus from any unwanted detractions, just as with the children brought to Jesus.[232] And it is possible, since Peter, James, and John seemed to comprise Jesus's innermost group, he had grown confused as to his role in the Lord's little band of followers, so he had comes to think bringing people to Jesus was not his job.

Any such reasoning at this point is only fruitless speculation, although we tend to make similar excuses in our own relationship with Jesus. Like Phillip, in this instance, we are often timid when it comes to sharing the gospel. We may hang back in unspoken fear and allow others to do what we should be doing; which is telling people about Jesus Christ. In any case, Phillip sought help from Andrews, the brother of Simon Peter.

Andrew also had a record of bringing people to Jesus. When he first met Jesus, Andrew found his brother Peter and brought him to Jesus.[233] He later stumbled onto the little boy who had the five loaves and two fish that Jesus used to feed the five thousand men, plus their families.[234] So together Andrew and Philip took these Greek men to see Jesus.

As it has already been stated, **we too are to bring people to Jesus.** It should be our goal in life that people come to know Jesus personally. Nothing should keep us from doing this—not our self-pity, not a misplaced sense of duty, and certainly not our prejudice. Sunday morning at the eleven o'clock hour should not be the most segregated hour in our nation. The gospel is for everyone regardless of age, sex, race, or economics. Many places in God's Word make this quite clear. We are to be his witnesses[235] to the lost who are headed toward eternal destruction. This is to be our chief goal as we seek to serve and glorify Jesus. Everything else—how we live, how we handle sickness and suffering, our Bible study and prayer life—all have this aim in mind—to help us tell others about Jesus. Depending on how we live, we are witnesses either for Jesus Christ or against him. If God loved the world enough to send Jesus to die, we should love him enough to tell the world what Jesus has done for them. We should love our neighbors enough to demonstrate the love of Jesus before them.

John does not tell us if Jesus met with these unusual visitors, but assuming he did, the Lord greeted them with words filled with wonder and mystery.

> The hour has come for the Son of Man to be glorified. (John 12:23)

"The hour has come." What hour? **The time for his sacrifice had come.** There can be little doubt that our Lord was referring to the time of his arrest, trials, and suffering on the cross. Up until this time, Jesus's hour had always been a future event.[236]

There is some debate among scholars as to when this meeting occurred. I would suggest it occurred sometime during the next couple of days after our Lord's triumphant entrance into the city of

Jerusalem on Sunday when he came—not as a conquering king—but as a humble servant riding on a young donkey.[237] Definitely not the way most people expect the Messiah to enter the city. At this point, his arrest in the garden and his various trials, as well as the crucifixion of our Lord at Calvary, were just a few days away. The course of events leading to the cross had already been set in motion. Indeed, such had been the case since the beginning of time,[238] and it had been often described down through the ages by the prophets. At his birth king Herod sought to kill him.[239] From the first day of his ministry in Nazareth, some opposed his teaching and sought to kill Jesus.[240] He was destined to die at the hands of sinful men just as he had told the disciples plainly on several occasions.[241] The religious leaders were already plotting to have him killed as soon as the opportunity presented itself.[242] In addition, it seems that Judas may have already begun to entertain the idea of betraying Jesus.[243] So the final events had already been set into motion, and nothing could prevent them. The clock was counting down to his death, and Jesus would do nothing to stop it. In fact, his confrontations with the religious leaders during the week leading to his arrest and crucifixion just seemed to ensure that it would happen.

The simple truth is that the Lord's death was necessary to fulfill the Father's plan for the salvation of humankind. In just a moment, God the Father responded to his Son's troubled prayer for help to complete his redemptive work[244] by speaking from heaven: "I have both glorified it, and I will glorify it again" (John 12:28 NASB). Jesus the Son of God was not alone, but his Father was present even in the middle of his emotional struggle over his coming ordeal. Once again, the Lord's explanation foretold his death in such cryptic terms that the disciples completely missed their significance.

> This voice came, not for me, but for you. Now is the judgment of this world. Now the ruler of this world will be cast out. As for me, if I am lifted up

from the earth I will draw all people to myself.
(John 12:30–32)

This is the third time God had spoken from heaven to be heard by humans,[245] but it's the only time mentioned by John. On this occasion, he spoke to bring humans' focus upon Jesus and to verify the message that he had come into the world to save humankind from their sin. "The Son of man was glorified by being crucified!"[246] The judgment of Satan and the sin was at hand. As he was lifted on the cross, Jesus proclaimed to the world the Father's redemptive plan by freely giving of his life in the most horrible way known to man. Through his resurrection the heavenly Father declared the Son's perfect obedience to that plan. Earlier the Lord Jesus Christ had said to his disciples after meeting the Samaritan woman at the well: "My food … is to do the will of him who sent me and to finish his work" (John 4:34 NIV). In the fifth chapter of John he said, "Verily truly I tell you, the Son can do nothing by himself; he can do only what he sees the Father doing … I myself can do nothing; … for I seek not to please myself, but him who sent me" (John 5:19, 30 NIV).

Jesus came to earth to seek and to save the lost. Throughout his earthly ministry, he was completely obedient to the heavenly Father's plan to bring judgment upon Satan and sin by defeating death and the grave. When Adam disobeyed God and ate of the forbidden fruit, he brought sin into the world and the curse of sin, which is death upon all humankind.[247] But Jesus Christ came into this world to declare God's great love and take upon himself all of our sin, as well as our punishment and the curse of death, so that by faith in him we might receive God's free gift of cleansing forgiveness and eternal life.[248]

Oh, that we would grasp the awfulness of our sin before a holy and just God. That we would truly comprehend the terrible price the Lord paid that we might be redeemed from Satan's snare and that we might comprehend the fullness of God's unmatchable grace and undeserved forgiveness. Oh, that this would motivate us to live lives worthy of his love and his grace and his mercy. Oh, that as we come to him that our lives would be completely transformed by the power of the Holy Spirit, and day by day we would yield ourselves unto Jesus Christ. That we would every moment of every day in every way surrender ourselves unto Jesus Christ the glorified Lord of heaven and earth.

Only through his death on the cross is there life eternal. By taking an example from the everyday life of this agrarian-based society, Jesus pointed to a remarkable event in a way that everyone understood.

> Truly I tell you, unless a grain of wheat falls to the ground and dies, it remains by itself. But if it dies, it produces much fruit. (John 12:24)

Stated another way, for a crop of grain to be produced, the seed that is planted in the ground must die. It must give up its life; its existence as a seed—so that new plants might sprout forth, grow, and produce a new crop.

With these simple words, Jesus was pointing to an even greater spiritual truth, which at this moment completely escaped the understanding of the Greeks and the disciples. It was a truth they were unprepared to hear or understand, but it would be revealed after his death and resurrection. Jesus was saying that he had to die and arise so that all humankind might be saved. It was only by Jesus freely dying on the cross as a perfect, sinless man that he could become the means by which we are saved. The apostle Paul explained further in the fifth chapter of Romans that "through one act of righteous there resulted justification of life for all men ... through the one man's obedience the many were made righteous" (Romans 5:18–19 NASB).

In obedience to God the Father, Jesus came into this world for a specific purpose. He came to live a sinless life—a righteous life—before God, to die on a cross at the hand of sinful man, and to arise from the grave on the third day. He came to die so that by faith in him we might be rescued from a life of sin and rebellion against God. Through the Lord's death on the cross, he paid the penalty for all our sin. By his resurrection we are assured that God stands ready to forgive all our sin if we will but confess our sin and turn from our wicked ways. Because of our belief in his sacrifice and his resurrection, we can stand before a Holy God covered with the sinless righteousness of Jesus and be called the sons of God.

Summing it up in a few words, Paul expressed it this way to Timothy: "Christ Jesus came into the world to save sinners—and I am the worst of them" (1 Timothy 1:15). Paul fully understood why Jesus Christ came into the world—to save all humankind. The very thought of the Lord's sacrifice dominated his every thought and action. His encounter with the glorified Christ on the road to Damascus[249] had so transformed him that he no longer sought to persecute the followers of Jesus but to call other men and women to be followers of Jesus. The Lord's great majesty and love compelled the apostle Paul to yield his life completely to him. His newfound relationship with Jesus Christ carried him through all the hard days of suffering and persecution and brought him a joy beyond human comprehension from the very throne of heaven. In Colossians he declared, "He has delivered us from the domain of darkness and transferred us to the kingdom of his beloved Son, in whom we have redemption, the forgiveness of sins" (Colossians 1:13–14 ESV). In Romans we find these words: "Christ died and returned to life for this: that he might be Lord over both the dead and the living" (Romans 14:9).

Not only is the sacrifice of Jesus on the cross necessary for the salvation of the world, but believers everywhere must also be willing to sacrifice everything in service to the Lord. Expounding on the Master's teaching, Paul expressed it this way: "What you sow does not come to life unless it dies. ... So it is with the resurrection of the dead: Sown in corruption, raised in incorruption; sown in dishonor, raised in glory; sown in weakness, raised in power; sown a natural body, raised a spiritual body. If there is a natural body, there is also a spiritual body." (1 Corinthians 15:36, 42–44). Although Jesus was focusing upon his own life, his teaching reminds us that "God does call some believers to die for him. But he calls many more to stay alive for fruitful service."[250] [251]

As difficult as it may be to understand, **only through self-abasement do we follow him**. This is another of the paradoxes we find quite often in the utterances of the Lord. *The New Living Bible* translates it this way:

> Those who love their life in this world will lose it.
> Those who care nothing for their life in this world
> will keep it for eternity. (John 12:25 NLT)

Let's begin by breaking down the Master's words so we might better understand what he means regarding our commitment to him. First, notice Jesus says, "The one who loves his life will lose it." How is this possible?

Think with me for a moment what we love about life. Let's start with the obvious. We love our families—our wives and husbands, our sons and daughters, our fathers and mothers, our grandchildren, and even our aunts and uncles. Then there are other people we might add to the list—friends, coworkers, and so forth. We love, well, life itself with all its challenges and mysteries, the hopes and dreams, and the adventures and successes. We love this great big beautiful world that God has created and set in motion for our provision, protection, and enjoyment. When we think about it and don't allow the evil around us to overcome us, there are a great many things about life that we enjoy and love. But notice Jesus says that if we loved life in this world more than him, we will lose it.

Based on scripture, it bears repeating once again. Everything we know in this life is temporal. It will not last. Life itself is but a vapor, the psalmist tells us.[252] Echoing the same thought, James wrote: "How do you know what your life will be like tomorrow? Your life is like the morning fog—it's here a little while, then it's gone" (James 4:14 NLT). If we accept this as truth, what will last? The answer is: only the things of God. That is why Jesus says, "The one who hates his life in this world will keep it for eternal life" (John 12:25). Once again, by using the word "hate" Jesus is seeking to make an important point for our benefit. Jesus is *not*, I repeat, *not* calling upon us to hate ourselves and harm ourselves in any way. Looking elsewhere in scripture, we find Jesus saying somewhat the same thing, but with slightly different words. In Matthew 10, we read:

> Anyone who finds his life will lose it, and anyone who loses his life because of me will find it. (Matthew 10:39)

In the sixteenth chapter of Matthew, he said,

> Whoever wants to save his life will lose it, but whoever loses his life because of me will find it. (Matthew 16:25)

In Luke 17, we discover these words from our Lord:

> Whoever tries to make his life secure will lose it, and whoever loses his life will preserve it. (Luke 17:33)

In each instance, the Lord's point is that he must be the primary focus of our lives, and not our family, our possessions, our positions, or anything in the arena where we live our daily lives. He must claim first place in every area of our lives. We are to give everything that we love—every member of our family, all our possessions, all our money and talents, all our positions of authority and power—unto

Jesus. If we are to serve him, we must devote our time, energy, and efforts unto him. Everything in our lives must be freely given unto him without any reservation. Anything less than total surrender and commitment on our part leaves us facing an uncertain future. It leaves us searching for a false hope and joy in things that will disappear. But God is eternal, and the riches and blessings he bestows on us are eternal.

During his life, George Muller exercised a wide influence for God. When someone asked him, "What has been the secret of your life?" Muller hung his head and said, "There was a day when I died." Then he bent lower and said, "Died to George Muller—his opinions, preferences, tastes, and will. Died to the world—its approval or censure. Died to the approval or blame even of brethren or friends."[253]

Have you died completely to self? If the truth be known, I am still working on this. And every time I think I have arrived—poof! Out of nowhere my old self rears its ugly head, and I must start all over again by confessing my sin and repenting of my arrogance. It is a daily struggle made easier through time spent with God in Bible study and prayer. Only by the power of the Holy Spirit can we overcome the daily temptations we face. Praise the Lord that victory over self comes through Jesus Christ.

Our Willing Service

A recently married man loved his young bride intensely. He wanted to provide her with the best home, nicest clothes, and everything else she might want. Though he had to hold down two jobs to do so, he did not mind, because they enabled him to provide for her many good things. Time together was hard to schedule, but he figured that later, once they were set financially, there would be plenty. Yet, as so often happens, within a few years his wife left him, not for more money or material things, but for a man who would spend time with her.

We often serve God and obey him, expending much time and energy in doing things that we believe will please him. But this is not enough. God wants us to know him intimately. We develop a relationship through the time we must spend with him.[254] His desire is that we worship him in spirit and truth and that we serve only him.[255] Look at the words uttered by Jesus:

> If anyone serves me, he must follow me. Where I am, there my servant also will be. If anyone serves me, the Father will honor him. (John 12:26)

Three ideas are present here. First, **when we follow Jesus, we serve only Jesus.** Please allow me to illustration this point. When Dr. W. A. Criswell, pastor of [what was at that time] the largest Southern Baptist church in the world, was preaching in the North Shore Baptist Church in Chicago, he was entertained at the home of deacon James L. Kraft, who was superintendent of the Sunday school and founder of Kraft Foods. Kraft said that as a young man he had a desire to be the most famous manufacturer and salesman of cheese in the world. He planned on becoming rich and famous by making and selling cheese and began as a young fellow with a little buggy pulled by a pony named Paddy. After making his cheese, the youth would load his wagon, and he and Paddy would drive down the streets of Chicago to sell the cheese. As the months passed, the young Kraft began to despair because he was not making any money despite his long hours and hard work.

One day he pulled his pony to a stop and began to talk to him. He said, "Paddy, there is something wrong. We are not doing it right. I am afraid we have things turned around, and our priorities are not where they ought to be. Maybe we ought to serve God and place him first in our lives." Kraft then drove home and made a covenant that for the rest of his life he would first serve God and then would work as God directed.

Many years after this, Dr. Criswell heard James Kraft say, "I would rather be a layman in the North Shore Baptist Church than to head the greatest corporation in America. My first job is serving Jesus."[256]

According to John 12:26, who are we to serve? Jesus Christ. Our task on this earth is not to serve ourselves but to serve Jesus. It is not even to serve others, but Jesus Christ. For some, the last statement is difficult to understand. "Can't we serve Jesus by serving others?" one may ask. Yes, we can, and we should, but herein also lays the problem. In our enthusiasm, we may become inclined to focus on one and forget the other. The truth is that we can get so caught up in serving others that before we realize it, we have left Jesus completely out of our efforts, and perhaps our lives. Without Jesus, we are simply good people doing good things, and no one is brought to Jesus. In our efforts to help others physically, we sometimes forget that we also must help them spiritually.

A few years ago, I experienced this during a mission event in the church where I was the pastor. As I was talking with a lady about Jesus Christ, someone came up and interrupted our conversation with some clothing I can only assume the lady had asked about earlier. Immediately the focus turned from Jesus to a single piece of clothing. The ultimate result was that I was unable to complete our conversation. Jesus and the message of salvation was replaced with the good intention of meeting a physical need, but the spiritual need was forgotten in the process. Both needs may have been met with just a little patience and thought.

Yes, the circumstance often requires that we meet a person's physical need before he or she is ready to hear the gospel. But sharing Jesus must always be our fundamental goal. Loving God and our neighbor requires that we help others, even at great personal expense. As a follower of Jesus, we cannot merely sit on the sidelines and wish someone well. During my ministry, I have also dealt with people who refused to help others by offering a well-worn catalog of reasons why specific people could not be helped or did not deserve our help. What can I say but that this is so unlike Jesus Christ.

James, the brother of Jesus, went to great pains to make this clear in his discussion about faith and works.[257] The example of the early church was of helping and giving in Christlike love over and over again. This is how Jesus lived his earthly life. He was always reaching out to help someone at the point of their greatest need. Likewise, we must learn that serving Jesus often means serving others. It involves showing the same compassion Jesus had for the multitudes and seeking ways to become involved in the lives of the individuals even when the circumstances are messy, and they make us uncomfortable. This will not always be easy or convenient. It will cost us something. But serving Christ by serving others should never cost us our witness for Christ.

Moreover, ministers of the gospel cannot escape this discussion. After nearly forty years in the gospel ministry, there have been times I have also been guilty of serving humans rather than God. There have been occasions when it was easier to give in to the pressures of the ministry and focus on preparing messages; attending meetings; visiting the sick, the lost, and the bereaved; and dealing with simpler problems that I begin to neglect my personal devotional life. "That's okay," one might say. "After all, we're serving God." The problem is that in time one's personal relationship with the Lord so declines that one becomes powerless for Christ. In turn, we become worn out physically, emotionally, and spiritually because we are too busy serving Christ to spend time with him. It is easy to forget that Jesus said, "Come to me, all of you who weary and burden, and I will give you rest" (Matthew 11:28–30). Serving Christ—doing good things for the Lord—can gradually lead us away from the very Master we claim to serve and need so badly in our lives. My brother or sister in Christ, what is true of a minister can be true of anyone who seeks to serve Jesus. Who are you serving—the Lord Jesus Christ or humans?

Writing to the church, Paul challenged each one of us, saying, "Whatever you do, whether in word or in deed, do it all in the name of the Lord Jesus, giving thanks to God the Father through him" (Colossians 3:17 NIV). Just a few verses later, Paul repeated the charge: "Whatever you do, work at it with all from the heart, as working for the Lord, not for human masters ... It is the Lord Christ you are serving" (Colossians 3:23–24 NIV).

Please understand this does not remove the need to maintain a spirit of love and unity within the congregation. It does not call for the pastor to become a bully to accomplish what he sees as God's will. Nor does it mean the church ignores the pastor's leadership to protect decades of traditions. Rather, it demands a spirit of discernment by all involved in order to determine what issues and ministries are of utter importance to the proclamation of the gospel. It implores all participants to sustain a willingness to seek harmony and agreement in everything that does not compromise biblical doctrine. Love and unity among God's people must be paramount lest our division become a stumbling block to our weaker brethren, as well as the unsaved. It calls for the leadership to keep Jesus Christ at the forefront of everything within the local body of believers.

My brothers and sisters in Christ, we are to serve Jesus Christ. Our task on this earth is not to serve ourselves but to serve Jesus. We are not to serve others but to serve Jesus. We are to give him our all. Our service is to the Lord Jesus and no one else. Five times in our scripture Jesus speaks of himself using the words: "me ... me ... I ... my ... me." These personal pronouns make it clear that when we follow Jesus, we serve only Jesus. The interesting part is this: when we seek with all our hearts to serve Jesus, we will also serve others out of the same love and compassion he has for them.

Furthermore, may we never forget that **only Jesus Christ is worthy of our worship and service.** He is worthy because he is the unblemished and spotless Lamb of God who takes away the sin of the world.[258] Jesus so perfectly obeyed the Father's will and died that "whosoever believeth in him might have eternal life" (John 3:16). God "made the One who did not know sin to be sin for us" (2 Corinthians 5:21). As the Son of God, he came to this world to give his life as a sacrifice on the cross of Calvary to rescue humans from the power of sin.[259] Then he arose to conquer death and the grave to give us hope of eternal life. Even now he is at the right hand of the Father ready to return and claim his followers and establish his eternal kingdom. No one else, no matter how great he or she may have been, is worthy of our worship and praise.

In addition, Jesus Christ is worthy of our service because God declared him worthy. In the immortal words of the apostle Paul,

> For this reason God highly exalted him
> and gave him the name
> that is above every name,
> so that at the name of Jesus
> every knee will bow
> in heaven and on earth
> and under the earth—
> and every tongue will confess
> that Jesus Christ is Lord,
> to the glory of God the Father. (Philippians 2:7–12)

All that Jesus accomplished on earth was done to bring glory to God the Father, and God the Father glorified him. Once again, what did God say from heaven? "I have glorified it, and I will glorify it again" (John 12:28). The Lord Jesus Christ completely glorified the Lord God here on earth by perfectly fulfilling his Father's divine plan through his death and resurrection that God glorified Jesus's name on earth before all humankind. "He is the focus of worship (Lord) and the administrator of God's will on earth."[260]

Please understand this. When we serve men, we become concerned about what men will think—how they will react, what they might say, or how we appear in their eyes. We become concerned about the rewards we might receive for our efforts from men. This can so dominate our thoughts and actions that it prevents us from serving Jesus as we should. When we are overly concerned about men—and even ourselves—we become distracted, and our focus is no longer upon the only one who is truly worthy—the Lord Jesus Christ. As a result, we give him less than our best as we strive to fulfill the pleasures and pressures of the world. But when we follow Jesus, we endeavor at every moment to walk closer to him. When we serve Jesus with all our hearts, minds, souls, and strength, our focus is on pleasing him, on honoring him, and on glorifying him. Our concern is for what the Lord might think about our service. Our desire is to give him our very best in everything we do.

In a fictional story, A. E. Whitham has an imaginary preacher give the following report of a visit to the New Jerusalem in our Lord's future earthly kingdom:

> In my wandering, I came upon the museum in the city of our dreams. I went in, and an attendant conducted me round. There was some old armor there, much bruised with battle. Many things were conspicuous by their absence. I saw nothing of Alexander's or of Napoleon's. There was no pope's ring, nor even the ink bottle that Luther is said to have thrown at the devil. I saw a widow's mite and the feather of a little bird. I saw some swaddling clothes, a hammer and three nails and a few thorns. I saw a sponge that had once been dipped in vinegar and a small piece of silver. Whilst I was turning over a simple drinking cup, which had a very honorable place, I whispered to the attendant: "Have you got a towel and basin among your collection?"

"No," he said, "not here. You see, they are in constant use."[261]

Swaddling clothes, a hammer, nails and thorns remind us of the loving service to the Father that Jesus offered as he came to die on our behalf. Likewise, the towel and basin call to mind how Jesus humbled himself and washed the disciples' feet at the final supper and his command to them to go and do likewise.[262]

When we humbly serve our Lord, everything else in the world fades into the shadows. Our focus is upon him, and we are willing to perform any service in his name no matter how demanding or humiliating it may be to us personally. We serve the Lord Jesus Christ because we know we are loved by him, and in turn, we love him. And out of his love, we love and serve others.

Moreover, when as we follow our Lord, he offers this assurance: "where I am, there my servant also will be" (John 12:26). **As his followers, we are assured of his presence.** A few days later while around the table in the upper room, Jesus said in very similar words to his disciples:

> In My Father's house are many mansions; if it were not so, I would have told you. I go to prepare a place for you. And if I go and prepare a place for you, I will come again and receive you to myself; that where I am, there you may be also. (John 14:2–3 NKJV)

He would later reaffirm this hope in his prayer for all believers, saying, "Father, I want these whom you have given me to be with me where I am. Then they can see all the glory you gave me because you loved me even before the world began!" (John 17:24 NLT).

The ultimate place we will experience the presence of our Lord is in our eternal home. In our celestial home, we will receive the blessing of being in his presence and seeing his face forever and ever. This is our blessed hope. But these words also hold great meaning for us in the present as we live on earth. As a follower of Jesus, we have the promise that his ever-present Spirit will be with us every day in whatever may come our way. "Lo, I am with you alway, even until the end of the world" (Matthew 28:20 KJV).

On the fateful night of his arrest, Jesus also issued another statement of fact to give encouragement to his disciples in the coming days. He said, "I am the vine; you are the branches. The one who remains in me, and I in him produces much fruit, because you can do nothing without me" (John 15:5).

Notice the final phrase of the verse: "you can do nothing without me" (John 15:5). Stated a little differently, but I believe accurately, it goes this way: "you can do nothing without the Holy Spirit." Both readings indicate the impossibility of doing God's work without his presence. The truth is—if we attempt to do the Master's bidding without his presence, we are depending on our own human abilities and resources; and our efforts, although well intended, are in vain.

We must never forget that it is by the power of the Spirit of God that individuals are drawn to God and saved. Remember Jesus said to Nicodemus, "Truly, truly, I say to you, unless one is born again, he cannot see the kingdom of God … Unless one is born of water and the Spirit he cannot enter into the kingdom of God" (John 3:3, 5 NASB). Similarly, under the guidance of the Holy Spirit, Paul wrote to believers in Rome that "the Spirit of God lives in you. … and if the Spirit of him who raised Jesus from the dead lives in you, he who raised Christ from the dead will also bring your mortal bodies to life through his Spirit who lives in you" (Romans 8:9, 11). Salvation itself is the work of the Holy Spirit. He is the "seal of ownership on us, and … in our hearts as a deposit, guaranteeing" that we are children of the heavenly Father (2 Corinthians 1:22 NIV). In response, we are to "walk in the Spirit" (Galatians 5:16) and "be filled with the Spirit" (Ephesians 5:18).

Likewise, the church was born by the power of the Holy Spirit. It was the Spirit who gave Peter the wisdom from the scriptures to proclaim with power "Jesus" before the people on that great day at Pentecost.[263] And it was the Lord through his Spirit who "added to their number those who were being saved" (Acts 2:47). It was the Spirit who gave Peter and John the boldness to preach the gospel before the Jewish Sanhedrin. Later, after they were flogged and released from jail, the Spirit enabled them to rejoice "that they were counted worthy to suffer shame for his name" (Acts 5:41 NKJV).

Similarly, Stephen, "full of the Holy Spirit, gazed into heaven and saw the glory of God, and Jesus standing at the right hand of God" (Acts 7:55), when his testimony so angered the religious leaders that they drove him out of the city and stoned him. The Spirit enabled him to forgive his murderers and peacefully die.[264] As these and so many other events in Acts show us, we can do nothing without the presence of the Holy Spirit.

On the eve of our Lord's crucifixion, he said to his befuddled disciples:

> When the Counselor comes, the one I will send to you from the Father—the Spirit of truth who proceeds from the Father—he will testify about me. You also will testify, because you have been with me from the beginning. (John 15:26–27)

We can serve our Lord Jesus Christ because the Holy Spirit dwells within us.[265] When we are weak, "the Spirit … helps us in our weakness." When we find it difficult to pray, he "intercedes for us with unspoken groaning … according to the will of God" (Romans 8:26–27). In his faithfulness, God "will not allow you to be tempted beyond what you are able, but … [by his Spirit] … he will provide a way out so that you may be able to bear it" (1 Corinthians 10:13). It is through the Spirit that we "receive mercy and find grace to help in time of need" (Hebrews 4:16). Even the special abilities and gifts we use in service to our Lord are given us by the Spirit.[266] The presence of the Spirit gives us the assurance that we are children of God.[267] One commentator summed it up with these words: "Wise men value greatly the Divine presence."[268]

Every day we are to make every effort to heed Paul's command: "If we live in the Spirit, let us also walk in the Spirit" (Galatians 5:25 KJV). This prompts us to be ever mindful to obey the apostle's warning—"Do not grieve Holy Spirit of God" (Ephesians 4:30 ESV). As believers we must always remember that "he saved us …

according to his mercy—through the washing of regeneration and renewal by the Holy Spirit … so that, having been justified by his grace, we may become heirs with the hope of eternal life" (Titus 3:5–7). Let us never forget that we are "justified in the name of the Lord Jesus Christ and by the Spirit of our God" (1 Corinthians 6:11). "For it is by grace you have been saved, through faith—and this is not from yourselves, it is the gift of God—not by works, so that no one can boast" (Ephesians 2:8–9 NIV).

Finally, Jesus goes on to say:

> If anyone serves me, the Father will honor him.
> (John 12:26)

As we have seen before, **followers of Jesus will be honored by God the Father.** Although Paul stated it differently in Colossians, he said much the same thing.

> Whatever you do, do it from the heart, as something done for the Lord and not for people, knowing that *you will receive the reward of an inheritance from the Lord.* You serve the Lord Christ. (Colossians 3:23–24) [Italic added for emphasis.]

My friends, we can focus on earthly rewards, but they are temporal at best. Even if our earthly rewards are not stolen or destroyed, at our death, we cannot take them with us. But the greatest reward any one of us can receive from the Lord Jesus Christ comes when we surrender everything unto him. On earth after salvation, we know his continual presence as we strive to serve him. The Bible speaks of other ways God honors all who follow Jesus. James declares that the one "who remains steadfast under trial … will receive the crown of life, which God has promised to those who love him" (James 1:12 ESV). Each of us has heard that heaven will be a place of great joy that is free from sin, death, mourning, crying, and pain.[269] In this life, we experience a little bit of heaven as we receive peace, hope, and love beyond imagination from his continual presence. In the life to come, we will stand in his presence and receive an indescribable eternal inheritance as coheirs with Christ. We will hear our Lord and God honor us with the words, "Well done my good and faithful servant! ... inherit the kingdom prepared for you from the foundation of the world" (Matthew 25:21, 34).

Finally, as a word of encouragement, Paul wrote to a persecuted people: "As for you, brothers and sisters, do not grow weary in doing good" (2 Thessalonians 3:13). Likewise, **we should not become discouraged in serving Christ.** In truth, this is easier said than done, especially when things are not going very well because we are facing criticism and personal attacks. The problem is that discouragement is one of the chief weapons Satan uses to disarm God's people and leave them powerless; therefore, we must never give in to its presence. We should never allow discouragement to lead us to second-guess our calling, our ministry, or our relationship to the Lord.

It is during such times that I have found it very important to keep my focus on Jesus Christ and remember we serve Jesus, not the whims of other people—because even good, godly people can be led astray. Sadly, this is often the result of a lack of faith in God and a failure to trust others, even among God's chosen leadership. Therefore, we must continually remind ourselves that we serve Jesus, not the desires of the powerbrokers among the church membership. We serve Jesus, not the special-interest groups within the congregation. We are to proclaim Jesus and him crucified to the best of our ability even though it may anger some within the fold. Yes, sometimes such individuals may be in alignment with God's will but not nearly as often as we are generally led to believe. The simple truth is that God's ways are routinely different than the world's way. After all, he has an eternal viewpoint. He sees the beginning and the end of every action and reaction. No one else can;

therefore, we must continually seek his face through Bible study and prayer for guidance. And when various opinions differ from God's path, we must stay the divine course and serve Jesus in the same spirit in which he served his Father.

The Bible says, "Serve with a good attitude, as to the Lord and not to people" (Ephesians 6:7). We can only do this by striving every day under the guidance of the Spirit to serve Jesus in love and humility. And when few respond to our faithful proclamation of the gospel, we still faithfully serve Jesus and keep on serving him as long as his call is upon us. Perhaps this is best illustrated by this story.

Many years ago, a humble pastor served a church in a little country town. His ministry was quiet, and few souls were brought to Christ there. Year in and year out, the work became more and more discouraging. It was only years later that the faithful minister found great joy in the knowledge that one of those he had won to Christ was Charles Haddon Spurgeon, a man who was later used by God to bring multitudes to his Son. Humble service is rewarded now and certainly will be rewarded even more when Christ comes.[270]

Are you humbly serving Jesus? Have you given yourself completely unto him?

Food for Thought

What did Jesus sacrifice for all humankind? Why is this important?

As followers of Jesus, who do we serve? Why?

As his servant, are you discouraged? If so, turn your face to Jesus. Read his word. Open an honest conversation with him in which you tell him what's going on in your life. Then stop, wait, and listen to his loving voice.

When [Judas Iscariot] had left, Jesus said, "Now the Son of Man is glorified, and God is glorified in him. If God is glorified in him, God will also glorify him in himself and will glorify him at once. Children, I am with you a little while longer. You will look for me, and just as I told the Jews, so now I tell you: 'Where I am going, you cannot come'" (John 13:31–33)

"Lord," Simon Peter said to him, "where are you going?"

Jesus answered, "Where I am going you cannot follow me now, but you will follow later."

"Lord," Peter asked, "why can't I follow you now? I will lay down my life for you."

Jesus replied, "Will you lay down your life for me? Truly I tell you, a rooster will not crow until you have denied me three times." (John 13:36–38)

CHAPTER 7

Why Can't I Follow You, Lord?

Having grandchildren is a wonderful experience, but there is never a dull moment. Some months ago, we were visiting our son and his family. As the clock moved toward four o'clock and because of the mounting afternoon traffic, my wife and I decided it was time to head home, so we began getting our things together. As we slipped on our coats and shoes, our two-year-old granddaughter came running and began putting on her shoes and coat. "Where are you going, sweetie," her mother asked?

"Go ga-ma, ga-pa," came the reply.

"But, honey, you can't go with them," her mother explained.

"Go ga-ma, ga-pa," she replied even more firmly as she tried in vain to slip her shoe on.

"But, sweetheart, you can't go with grandma and grandpa today."

For a third time, "Go ga-ma, ga-pa," she said with a sense of finality.

Each of us lovingly laughed at her growing insistence, and then Susan and I got down on our knees so we could hug her and assure her of our love. We tried to explain that she could not go right then, but we would work it out so she could go with us later. Our granddaughter was none too happy, but she stayed home without violently protesting our decision.

The Perfect Messiah

In the upper room we find a similar situation. Jesus has been with the disciples for three years. They have followed him throughout much of his earthly ministry, but now as his time on earth is coming to an end, the situation had changed dramatically. Only the Master's love for them had not changed. During an evening filled with wonder and mystery, Jesus washed the disciples' feet and celebrated the Passover. Then he began to prepare his disciples to endure the terrible events that were just a few hours away. After Judas exited the upper room to betray him, Jesus sat up, so he could see each one of them more clearly, and said with a sense of finality and purpose:

> Now the Son of Man is glorified, and God is glorified in him. ... Children, I am with you a little while longer. You will look for me, and just as I told the Jews, so now I tell you: "Where I am going, you cannot come. (John 13:32–33)

He then moved on to instruct them to "love one another. Just as I have loved you, you are also to love one another" (John 13:34). Such a love was to be "the distinguishing mark of discipleship" among the Lord's followers.[271] It is one of the themes repeatedly mentioned in his parting instruction to his disciples.[272] But it appears Simon Peter sought to sidestep this responsibility by focusing on the Master's statement "where I am going, you cannot come."[273] As Peter turned it over in his mind, the idea of Jesus leaving deeply disturbed him. Apparently, he did not understand what Jesus meant. So mystified, he asked, "Lord, ... where are you going?"

Let's stop at this point and focus on this inquiry. After all, Peter's question should be answered; it is too important to just glance over because Jesus spoke of his departure throughout the evening.[274] When he had brought this subject up to the religious leaders some time earlier, they did not understand either, so they chose to mock and condemn him.[275] But this is not the case with Peter. Although we cannot hear the tone of his voice, it appears he genuinely wanted to know—Where was Jesus going that he could not go?

Reading the gospel record concerning the coming events indicates that in the immediate sense, Jesus and his small band of followers were headed to a small garden on the Mount of Olives where Jesus often went to pray. But that was as far as most of them would go on this night. In a few hours, after Jesus had finished praying, Judas showed up with a mob consisting of armed soldiers, priests, and other Jewish officials to arrest him by the authority of the Jewish High Court. With his arrest most of the disciples deserted him. From this moment, things very quickly headed downhill as the Lord faced a series of reprehensible trials that lasted the rest of the night and into the early morning. The first three trials were before the Jewish religious leaders where his death sentence was already predetermined.[276] Jesus must die for the good of the Jewish nation, they had concluded a week or so earlier.[277] The final three trials were held with the rising of the morning sun in the eastern sky as he was tossed between Pilate, King Herod, and then back to Pilate. The tragic (but divinely appointed) results of all this was that he was unjustly convicted and sentenced as a common criminal to die on a cross. Although Pilate had found no fault in him, fearing the crowd, he surrendered to their cries and ordered Jesus crucified.[278] So by eight o'clock, Jesus was probably well down the road, which wandered through the streets of Jerusalem, to his crucifixion. At Golgotha, with nails in his hands and feet, he hung between two convicted thieves for six hours between heaven and earth, while he was mocked and insulted by many of the same mob that shouted for his death. For the last three hours, the sky turned black as night as the afternoon sun suddenly darkened over the whole land until, in utter exhaustion, he surrendered his spirit unto the Father.[279]

With his death sentence carried out, Jesus was quickly and quietly buried in a borrowed tomb by two members of the Sanhedrin who had apparently reminded silent followers until this moment.[280] But the time for silence was over as they publicly claimed his body and lovingly laid him in a borrowed tomb. And yet that does not begin to tell the whole story.

On the third day, Jesus miraculously arose from the dead—just as he predicted. As the sun was just making its appearance, a group of women were the first to discover his empty tomb. Having rolled the stone away from the entrance, the angels invited them to witness where he had been laid and then go tell his disciples. Rest assured, the tomb was empty, but his body had not been moved, nor had it been stolen. He had arisen from the dead. Throughout the day and those that followed, time after time he appeared bodily to his followers—in the garden, on the road to Emmaus, twice in the upper room, along the Sea of Galilee—to name a few. Each occasion served to encourage and assure his followers that he was alive! For forty days, he was often with them as he sought to further train and prepare his friends to become his witnesses to the world.[281]

And then, and only then, with his mission of redemption for all humankind finished, even as he spoke, Jesus rose up into the clouds as the disciples watched in wonder as he returned to his celestial home.[282] In heaven, he is even now preparing a place for all his followers throughout time[283] as he sits on the right hand of God the Father to intercede for them. The Bible further indicates that one day, at a time known only to the Father, the Lord Jesus Christ will return to receive his followers unto himself and reclaim this world as his kingdom from the forces of Satan. And then he will reign forever and ever and ever.

Yes, just as the Master had answered Peter, "Where I am going you cannot follow me now, but you will follow later," Jesus was going to a place his disciples could not follow at this time for several reasons.

First, **Jesus had a mission of love to complete for the Father.** It was a mission that no one else could complete. He had been sent by God the Father in the form of man for this specific purpose. In the third chapter of John we find these words: "For God so loved the world, that he gave his only begotten Son into the world ..." God the Father sent Jesus into the world for a specific purpose—"that the world through him might be saved" (John 3:16–17 KJV). Jesus declared after the salvation of Zacchaeus, "For the Son of Man has come to seek and to save the lost" (Luke 19:10). Paul wrote in his first letter to Timothy:

> It pleases God our Savior, who wants everyone to be saved and to come to the knowledge of truth. For there is one God and one mediator between God and humanity, the man Christ Jesus, who gave himself as a ransom for all. (1 Timothy 2:5–6)

Jesus came from God the Father into the world for a specific purpose. He came as a baby born in Bethlehem as "a Savior, who is Christ the Lord" (Luke 2:11). He lived and walked on this world for a specific purpose—to be tempted as we are so that he might encourage us and help us overcome our own temptations and trials.[284] He came so that we might know him and "grow in every way into ... Christ" (Ephesians 4:13). And now, in the upper room as he sat around the table with his disciples for one last time before his suffering, he pointed once again to that purpose, saying, "Where I am going, you cannot come." His unique purpose for coming into this world was to save all humanity by giving himself as a ransom for our sin. He came with a specific purpose—to die on a cross that men and women, boys and girls, old and young alike might be saved from the penalty of our sin.

In just a few hours, his great suffering would begin. In less than twenty-four hours, he would be physically dead after being victimized for most of the night by the Jewish religious leaders. Then he was mocked and brutally flogged with third-nine lashes from a Roman whip, which brought him to the very threshold of death. Finally, after having nails driven through his hands and feet, he suffered for six hours on the cross. Only after experiencing complete loneliness as the Father turned his face from him because he bore the sins of the world, did he cry out, "It is finished!" and give up the ghost and die (John 19:30). But he did not only come to die. He came to arise again on the third day.[285]

Just a few months earlier he had caused a stir among the Jews by saying:

> I am the good shepherd. I know my own, and my own know me, just as the Father knows me, and I know the Father. I lay down my life for the sheep. ... This is why the Father loves me, because I lay down my life so that I may take it up again. No one takes it from me, but I lay it down on my own. I have the right to lay it down, and I have the right to take it up again. I have received this command from my Father. (John 10:14–18)

By his own words, Jesus chose to lay "down his life" and died on the cross for our sin. But he also possessed power from God to "take it up again" and arise from the grave on the third day that we might have life eternal. Jesus was sent by God for a specific purpose—to redeem humankind from their sin.

In addition, **Jesus was the only Person who was uniquely qualified to fulfill God's purpose**. He is the only one who could completely fulfill God's mission of saving humankind—no one else could do so. Why, you may ask? Without getting caught up in all the arguments surround this thought, let's very quickly examine four reasons Jesus Christ is the only one qualified to be the Savior of the world.

First, Jesus is the only person to ever be completely obedient to

God the Father. A brief review of biblical history bears this out. In the beginning, as history began, God demanded perfect obedience from Adam and Eve, but they sinned, and the consequences of their lack of belief and disobedience involved death.[286] Paul declared in his letter to the Romans, "Just as sin entered the world through one man, and death through sin, in this way death spread to all people, because all sinned" (Romans 5:12). For this reason, just about everything that followed the sin of Adam and Eve was also corrupted by sin. The events surrounding the flood[287] and the tower of Babel[288] were the results of human sinfulness. Years later, as Moses led the Israelite nation from slavery in Egypt, their continual sin often brought God's judgment upon them—usually in the form of death. The book of Judges describes for us a time when "everyone did whatever seemed right to him" (Judges 17:6, 21:25), which "was evil in the Lord's sight" (Judges 2:11). During the days when the kings ruled the Jewish nation, we find continual rebellion and sin as the people forgot God and ignored his commands. In a similar fashion, even King David, Israel's greatest king, and Solomon, the wisest man to ever live, yielded to temptation and sinned against God. Could we expect any more from the other kings of Judah and Israel who made no pretense of following God's commands? Several times the Bible plainly made the statement that they "did evil in the sight of the Lord," and sadly, these kings also led the people to do evil in God's eyes. According to the Old Testament prophets, God punished the Jewish nation with captivity in Assyria and then in Babylon because of their continual rebellion and sin against him. Finally, in 70 AD, God used the Romans to punish once again his wayward people.

Looking back into Israel's history, the apostle Paul began the book of Romans, his great doctrinal statement on salvation, by saying: "Although they know God's righteous decree that those who do such things deserve to die" (Romans 1:32 NIV). Likewise, the Old Testament prophet Ezekiel clearly stated God's judgment: "The person who sins is the one who dies" (Ezekiel 18:20). Why do sinners deserve to die? Paul writes that it is because by "one man's disobedience the many were made sinners, so death spread to all people, because all sinned" (Romans 5:19). From the beginning of time, God wanted a loving relationship with humans, but they chose to reject him and sin against him. Since God is perfect holiness, his perfect judgment declared that all sin is punishable by death.

This brings us to an undeniable truth of scripture—that all humans are sinners. The Bible states, "There is no one righteous, not even one ... For all have sinned and fallen short of the kingdom of God" (Romans 3:10, 23). James made God's demand for perfect obedience even clearer as he wrote, "For whoever keeps the whole law and yet stumbles at one point, he has become guilty of all." A little later, he further added, "To one who knows the right thing to do and does not do it, to him it is sin" (James 2:10; 4:17 NASB). It is an inescapable truth; try as they might, humans cannot be perfectly obedient unto God.[289] Only Jesus was able to live perfectly in accordance to God's will. For this reason, only through "one man's obedience"—namely Jesus Christ—can "the many be made righteous" (Romans 5:19). The unavoidable fact is that Jesus is the only person in all of history to be completely obedient unto the LORD God.

Jesus said of himself,

> Truly I tell you, the Son is not able to do anything on his own, but only what he sees the Father doing. For whatever the Father does, the Son likewise does these things. ... I do not seek my own will, but the will of him who sent me. (John 5:19)

Throughout His life, Jesus sought only to fulfill the will of the Father, and by doing so, he was completely obedient unto the Father. It was this obedience that enabled him to perfectly fulfill the law and the prophets as no man has even been able to do. In his letter to the Philippians, Paul declared that because "he humbled himself by becoming obedient to the point of death—even death on the cross" God highly exalted his Son and gave him a name above every name (Philippians 2:8–9).

Furthermore, the Lord's complete obedience unto the will of the Father also means Jesus was entirely without sin. There was absolutely no sin in him because he did everything, absolutely everything, that the Father asked him to do—even die on the cross. In Corinthians, Paul stated, "God ... made the one who did not know sin to be sin for us, so that in him we might become the righteousness of God" (2 Corinthian 5:20–21). John wrote, "He appeared in order to take away sins, and in him there is no sin" (1 John 3:5, ESV). In his discussion of the great high priest, the writer of Hebrews declared, "This is the kind of high priest we need: holy, innocent, undefiled, separated from sinners, and exalted above the heavens" (Hebrews 7:26). This described Jesus perfectly. He "faced all of the same testing we do, yet he did not sin" (Hebrews 4:15 NLT). Jesus is the only one who has ever lived who remained without sin. But if Jesus was human like us, how was he able to live a sinless life?

His perfect obedience was possible because Jesus is the Son of God. Gabriel announced his birth to Mary declaring that her son "will be great and will be called the Son of the Highest" (Luke 1:32). At his baptism by John the Baptist, God declared in a voice from the heavens: "This is my beloved Son, with whom I am well-pleased" (Matthew 3:17). He spoke twice more, and each time the LORD God affirmed that Jesus was his Son.[290] Also, John 3:16 calls Jesus—God's "one and only Son." Finally, in the first chapter of Hebrews, we find this statement of fact:

> In these last days, *he has spoken to us by his Son.* God has appointed him heir of all things and made the universe through him. The Son is the radiance of God's glory and the exact expression of his nature, sustaining all things by his powerful word. After making purification for sins, he sat down at the

right hand of the Majesty on high. (Hebrews 1:2–3)
[Italic added for emphasis.]

When I was a teenager, I was challenged by our youth director to debate this topic: Did Jesus ever declare himself to be God? My assignment was to defend the idea that in the gospels he had declared himself to be God, while my best friend was to prove the opposite. For a young Christian of sixteen, the whole idea was way beyond my abilities. But years later it has become crystal clear that this was exactly who Jesus is. Not only is Jesus God's Son, but in a great mystery of God—Jesus Christ is God.

Did you notice how the author of Hebrews described Jesus? He is "the radiance of God's glory and the exact expression of [God's] nature" (Hebrews 1:3). In his letter to the Colossians, Paul explained that "he is the image of the invisible God, the firstborn over all creation ... God was pleased to have all his fulness dwell in him and through him to reconcile everything to himself" (Colossians 1:15, 19–20).[291] In the next chapter, he added, "The entire fullness of God's nature dwells bodily in Christ" (Colossians 2:9). These passages and others declare the uncompromising truth that in Jesus resides the "full nature of God." According to the footnote for this passage in the *Christian Standard Study Bible*, this means that "Jesus was fully divine as well as fully man."[292] In other words, Jesus is the living God "manifested in the flesh" (1 Timothy 3:1–15). In Revelation, Jesus declared to John the apostle, "I am the Alpha and the Omega ... the one who is, who was, and who is to come, the Almighty ... the beginning and the end" (Revelation 1:8; 21:6 NIV). All these are titles that can only apply to the everlasting God.

During the last year of his earthly ministry, Jesus stated as fact, "Truly I tell you, before Abraham was, I am" (John 8:58), and a few days later he added, "I and the Father are one" (John 10:30). Realizing that he was claiming to be God, the Jewish religious leaders were angered and "picked up rocks to stone him." In their eyes such a statement violated the law of Moses.[293] They saw the

Lord's words as a statement of "blasphemy, because you—being man—make yourself God" (John 8:59; 10:31–33). In fact, this was the same charge the high priest used to convict Jesus during his trial before the Sanhedrin.[294] On another occasion, Jesus was on a high mountain with Peter, James, and John meeting with the Old Testament prophets Moses and Elijah, when "he was transfigured in front of them, and his clothes became dazzling—extremely white." In that moment, by revealing the "radiance of God's glory," Jesus revealed his divine nature to the disciples. Also, the Father confirmed his identity by speaking from the heavens, saying in essence, "'This is my beloved Son; listen to him!' (Mark 9:2–10). His voice is my voice; his word is my word; his authority is my authority."

There are many other indications of his divinity. The Lord's divine authority to forgive sin was made evident on numerous occasions as it drew the anger of the Pharisees.[295] His ability to heal all kinds of sickness and handicaps,[296] as well as to control the wind, waves, and rain asserted his mastery over all of creation.[297] Before he silenced them, time after time the demons openly declared Jesus's divine nature.[298] Christ's dominance over life and death was made evident as he raised individuals from the dead;[299] as did his own death and resurrection. All of this and so much more has provided clear evidence that Jesus Christ was God making an appearance on earth. He came that humankind might experience and know him as never before. In order to save and redeem humans, the infinite holy God chose to reveal a tiny fraction of his divine, loving nature through Jesus Christ to humans. And even that teensy-weensy revelation of God is still far too great for the limited mind of mortals to grasp in any measure. The result is that some chose to blindly reject him, while others gave their lives to follow him. Paul declared that one reason humans cannot see "the light of the gospel of the glory of Christ" is because "the god of this age has blinded the minds of unbelievers" (2 Corinthians 4:4). In other words, our sinfulness has prevented us from recognizing the very limited portion of his majesty God has chosen to reveal to us through the Lord Jesus Christ.

So once again, why did Jesus come into the world? The apostle John wrote, "He was revealed so that he might take away sins" (1 John 3:5). The writer of Hebrews goes on to say,

> Now since the children have flesh and blood in common, Jesus also shared in these, so that through his death he might destroy the one holding the power of death—that is, the devil—and free those who were held in slavery all their lives by the fear of death. (Hebrews 2:14–15)

Jesus came to fulfill God's divine plan to redeem humans from their sin. He came into this world to live a perfect life and die on the cross as a perfect sacrifice, in order that the penalty for my sin and your sin might be paid in full. The Lord Jesus Christ came to reveal the holy and loving nature of God to a world that is filled with hated, violence, rebellion, and sin. He came for the purpose of saving us from our sinful condition and to redeem us from the death we rightly deserve. He came to offer us complete forgiveness for our sin and new life in him.

We see the divine plan played out at Calvary as "darkness came over the whole land [from noon] until three in the afternoon" (Mark 15:33). During this time, God the Father turned his face from his one and only Son. Why one may ask? It was because in that moment, Jesus literally bore the sins of every man, woman, and child who has lived or will live on this planet. God's total abandonment of his "sin-satiated" Son was revealed as Jesus cried out in torment that we can never comprehend, "My God, my God, why have you forsaken me?" (Mark 15:33–34). His death on the cross was the consequence of God's judgment upon the sin of all humankind. But death was not the end. Jesus arose so that in him we might have eternal life. Paul declared, "We know that Christ, having been raised from the dead, will not die again. Death no longer rules over him. For the death he died, he died to sin once for all time, but the life he lives, he lives to God. So, you too consider yourselves dead to sin and alive to God in Christ Jesus" (Romans 6:9–10). In the divine plan, Jesus Christ died and arose, so that by faith in him we might become new creatures in Christ and become alive to God for all eternity.

In our scripture his disciples could not follow him because Jesus Christ the God-man was on a divine mission to redeem all of humankind from sin. It was a mission only the sinless Lord Jesus Christ could complete. As we come to understand the importance of this, each of us could say with Paul, "Christ Jesus came into the world to save sinners—and I am the worst of them" (1 Timothy 1:15). My friend, will you come by faith to Jesus right now and be saved from your sin?

So why is it necessary for us to come by faith to Jesus? The reason is because **the Lord Jesus Christ is the only way to salvation.**

Just a few hours before he was arrested, Jesus declared to the disciples, "I am the way, the truth, and the life. No one comes to the Father but by me" (John 14:6). In other words, Jesus was saying that all humankind can only be saved by faith in him. I find it interesting that each time Jesus said, "I am" in John's gospel, he pointed to the words uttered by God to Moses from the burning bush: "I Am Who I Am" (Exodus 3:14). In other words, every single time Jesus said, "I am," he was speaking with the full authority and power of God the Father. This was possible because Jesus is God incarnate. The God of the Old Testament is the Savior and Lord of the New Testament come to earth to save humans.

Furthermore, when a confused Philip asked, "Lord … show us the Father," Jesus repeated similar words he had spoken to the religious leaders:[300] "Have I been among you all this time and you do not know me, Philip? The one who has seen me has seen the Father" (John 14:8–9). How is this possible? It is possible because "I

and the Father are one ... the Father is in Me and I in the Father"
(John 8:30, 38). Jesus is God come to earth in the flesh.

The beloved disciple began his gospel saying, "In the beginning
was the Word and the Word was with God and the Word was
God. ... The Word became flesh and dwelt among us." (John 1:1,
14). After a life of faith, John wrote: "We know that the Son of God
has come and has given is understanding so that we may know the
true one. We are in the true one—that is, in his Son Jesus Christ.
He is the true God and eternal life" (1 John 5:19, 20). Jesus was
and is God. Taking the form of man, God came into the world for
a specific purpose—to seek and save the lost. Therefore, only by
confessing "that Jesus Christ has come in the flesh is from God"
can anyone be saved (1 John 4:2–3).

This is a clear declaration of the Bible. Only by believing in the
God-man Jesus Christ can anyone be saved from his or her sin. This
is true of even the most moral and good people who have ever lived.
It is one of the reasons the divinity of Jesus has come under such
attack down through the ages. If Jesus is not divine, he cannot be
God, and if he is not God, he cannot save us from our sin. Moreover,
if salvation is not only through the Lord Jesus Christ, then there is
no need to believe in him, and there is no judgment. And if there
is no judgment, there is no punishment for sin, and humankind is
free to live according to his or her own sinful selfish desires without
any regard for God. But scripture declares that Jesus Christ is God;
therefore, belief in him is our only path to salvation. We do not have
to fully understand this mystery of God, but we must accept that
with God anything is possible. In the time in which we live, this is
no easy task because we have been taught to question everything,
especially spiritual things. That is why we must come to Jesus like
a child and believe in him with the simplicity of a child. We must
permit the Holy Spirit to speak to our spirit and then listen to his
loving voice calling us to salvation in Jesus Christ.

In the early days of the church, standing before the High Jewish
Court, the apostle Peter boldly stated, "There is salvation in no one

else, for there is no other name under heaven given to people by which we must be saved" (Acts 4:12). Weeks later Peter declared to a centurion named Cornelius, "everyone who believes in him [meaning Jesus] will have their sins forgiven through his name" and the Holy Spirit came down upon them offering divine prove that they believed in Jesus (Acts 10:43–44 NLT). In his letter to the Romans, Paul wrote, "If you confess with your mouth, 'Jesus is Lord,' and believe in your heart that God raised him from the dead, you will be saved. One believes with the heart, resulting in righteousness, and one confesses with the mouth, resulting in salvation. ... For everyone who calls on the name of the Lord will be saved" (Romans 10:9–10, 13).

Once again, we must believe in Jesus. He is the perfect Messiah. Only the holy Lord of heaven and earth can forgive our sin and save us. This is why God chose to come into the world in human form—to provide the only means through which we might be saved. It bears repeating. Only by faith in Jesus Christ can we be saved from our sin. My friend, will you come by faith in Jesus? Will you believe in the Lord Jesus Christ? He is the only way to salvation.

The Imperfect Disciples

Some years ago, my wife had an all-expense-paid three-day trip to Washington, DC. There she was to attend a conference involving high school teachers from across the nation. Since she had a room all to herself, I checked my calendar and made to plans to go along. After all, it meant we could spend some time away together, and I would only need to pay for our meals and for what we chose to do together. We had packed our bags and were loading them into the car when I received a call. A member of my congregation had passed away suddenly. In disappointment we removed my bag from the car, and Susan called her mother to attend the conference with her. Meanwhile, I spent the next few days ministering to the grieving family. In my disappointment, I was unable to go because I was needed at home.

No doubt disappointment also showed on the faces of the disciples as Jesus informed them that he was going away, and they would not be able to follow him. For three years they had been constant companions as Jesus led them throughout the countryside of Galilee and Judea. But his mission on earth had reached a crucial point. He was to travel a cruel path, which they could not for several reasons. As we have seen, two of the reasons related specifically to him. The first reason dealt with his mission of love for God the Father. He had come to earth in order to die and save lost men from their sin. The second reason focused on the fact that because Jesus Christ was both man and God, only he was uniquely qualified to fulfill God's purpose of providing a means by which humans could be save from their sin. Now let's turn our attention to five more reasons why the disciples could not follow Jesus.

First, his disciples could not follow Jesus because **God had other plans for them.** In respond to the statement by the Lord, Peter declared—in the moment with all the conviction he could muster: "[But] Lord, … why can't I follow you now? I will lay down my life for you" (John 13:37). What a magnificent boast by Peter! Yes, there would be a day when Peter would lay down his life for Jesus—but not that night. God had other plans for him. Somewhere along the way to the garden, Jesus stopped and prayed:

> I am no longer in the world, but they are in the world, and I am coming to you. Holy Father, protect them by your name that you have given me, so that they may be one as we are one. While I was with them, I was protecting them by your name that you have given me. I guarded them, and not one of them is lost, except the son of destruction, so that the Scripture may be fulfilled. (John 17:11–12)

While he was on earth, the disciples were under the protection of the Son of God. When he commissioned the disciples to go out in his name, he instructed them not to fear humankind but to fear God.[301] Later as he sent the seventy-two followers out to witness and proclaim his coming, Jesus assured them, "Nothing at all will harm you" (Luke 10:19). Now with his departure just days away, the disciples would be under the protection of God the Father, and what greater protection is there? Further proof that it was not their time to die can be found in the Lord's request in the garden to those who came to arrest him: "I have told you that I am He. Therefore, if you seek Me, let these go their way" (John 18:8 NKJV). And they let the disciples go free.

Death would find the disciples at later times. Tradition tells us that after years of proclaiming Jesus as the Savior of the world, Peter died as a blind old man in Rome during the reign of Nero hanging upside down on a cross because he was unworthy to die as his Lord had. Likewise, in the days to come most of the other disciples would also be killed for the sake of the gospel. But until death called them home, Jesus had different plans for each of them. The men gathered around the table with the Lord were to be his future messengers to the world. Their part in the divine plan was still to come. They were to set in motion the fulfillment of the Great Commission.[302] They were to go to all the world and teach and train other individuals about Jesus, so that they too might share the message of the gospel with other people, who would do likewise. Their divinely assigned task in the plan of God had not yet even begun. On the day of Pentecost, we see the Holy Spirit coming down upon these followers of Jesus with such power that in great boldness they fearlessly declared Jesus before those gathered for the festival. The entire book of Acts accounts the beginnings of the proclamation of the gospel of Jesus Christ to the world. And that same task has been passed down through the ages to us. As his followers, in our time and place, we are now the divinely appointed couriers of the message of the gospel of Jesus Christ. Our part in the divine plan is also to tell others about Jesus. Like the disciples of old, we are to go to all the world and teach and train other individuals about Jesus, so that they too might share the message of the gospel with other people, who would in turn go and teach and share the gospel message.

A fictional story is told of when Jesus ascended to heaven after his mission on earth, and the angels asked him, "Did you accomplish your task?"

"Yes, all is finished," the Lord replied.

"We have a second question," said the angels. "Has the whole world heard of you?"

"No," said Jesus.

The angels next asked, "Then what is your plan?"

Jesus said, "I have left twelve men and some other followers to carry the message to the whole world."

The angels looked at him and asked, "What is your plan B?"

Friends, there is no plan B. In his eternal wisdom Jesus has chosen to reach the world through men and women like you and me.[303]

Just as the Lord had a plan for the disciples, he has a plan for us. We are to go into all the world and declare Jesus Christ crucified and risen. Then, as the Holy Spirit draws them unto the Father, we are to teach them the mysteries of gospel and help them grow in the knowledge of Jesus Christ, in order that they too might go forth and declare Jesus to the world and teach others how to grow in Christ, so they might share Jesus with other people. After more than two thousand years, the mission is not yet complete. Billions have only heard a one-sided, incomplete, and even untrue message about Jesus. As with the first disciples, it is our task to declare the truth of Jesus Christ to the world.

There is a second reason they could not go with Jesus. As they sat around the table with the Lord, the truth of the matter was that **the disciples were not as committed as they claimed.** Peter claimed,

"I will lay down my life for you" (John 13:37). But seeing in his heart a mixture of loyalty and cowardice,[304] Jesus said to him, "Truly I tell you, ... a rooster will not crow until you have denied me three times." The Greek word for "denied" (*aparneomai*) meant "to deny utterly"—implying that Peter would deny Jesus in the most fierce and absolute terms available.[305] He would completely disavow Jesus as though he never had the least thing to do with him.[306]

Offended by the Lord's prediction, we are told in Mark's Gospel that Peter stubbornly kept insisting, "Even if everyone falls away, I will not ... If I have to die with you, I will never deny you." It almost sounds as if Peter was boasting about his great ability to follow Jesus. Not surprisingly, all the disciples, caught up in the moment, "said the same thing" (Mark 14:29–31). The sin of pride had once again reared its ugly head in Peter's life; and nothing could be further from the truth. The Lord's prediction would come to fruition in just a matter of hours. In answering Peter, Jesus dropped his second bombshell of the evening. Not only would Judas betray Jesus, but Peter would deny him.[307] William Barclay distinguishes between the betrayal of Judas and the denials of Peter noting, "The sin of Peter was the sin of a moment's weakness and a lifetime's regret."[308]

Before the night was over all eleven disciples fell asleep when they should have followed the example of Jesus—and prayed. As the mob arrested their Lord, all who had earlier claimed total commitment to Jesus deserted him in his time of greatest need. Yes, Peter rashly sought to defend Jesus with a sword. But when Jesus told him to put his sword away and healed the injured servant, the Lord probably stopped them from being massacred in a lopsided battle against the temple's trained soldiers.[309] Yes, Peter and John followed him even into the courtyard of the high priest. But we discover just how far his commitment went as we find Peter standing around the fire warming himself surrounded with men and women loyal to the high priest. There in the midst of those who arrested Jesus, when confronted, Peter denied Jesus, not once, not twice, but three times, just as Jesus had predicted.[310] As the "rooster crowed a second time" and the loving eye of the Lord fell upon him from across the courtyard, Peter remembered the vow he had made unto the Lord and fled the scene as he "broke down and wept" (Mark 13:72; Luke 22:61). And so, the next day at Calvary, only John could be found offering support to the Lord's mother, along with several other women, as they watched Jesus die a horrible death on the cross. Everyone else had deserted him—even Peter.

The simple truth is that the disciples were not as committed to Jesus as they claimed. They could only give lip service to their devotion because they were not yet fully prepared to make the ultimate sacrifice for their Lord. Apparently, they were confused and overwhelmed by the unexpected events surrounding Jesus's arrest, trials, and crucifixion. It appears the Lord's words of warning regarding his coming suffering at the hands of man were simple forgotten by the disciples. In the horror of a moment in time, three years of training by the Master just vanished from their thoughts. Nothing made sense. "What had just happened? How could it happen?" they must have asked. Like soldiers overcome by battle fatigue, they were so emotionally, mentally, and physically exhausted that they could do little more than hide in fear and weep for their loss.

My brothers and sister, before we criticize the disciples too harshly, we must ask ourselves, "Am I prepared to die for Jesus? How strong is my commitment to the Lord?" If we are honest, most of us would need to admit our level of commitment is no better than Peter's or any of the other nine disciples. At the very least, he walked on water. Have we ever done so?[311] So many times we are committed—unless something better or more interesting comes our way. We are willing to follow Jesus—if the path is not too demanding or too difficult. This is something we need to examine very carefully because I believe that a day is coming when we too will face persecution. This is what we have tried to address throughout this book. How committed are we to Jesus? How will we fare under the tribulation Christians in other nations face every day? Are we prepared to give him our all—and even die for Jesus? As our study has revealed, this is what taking up our cross daily for Jesus Christ demands.

In addition, they could not follow him because **the disciples had not been empowered by the Holy Spirit.** According to Jesus, the Spirit could not come until he returned to heaven, but "when the Counselor comes, the one I will send to you from the Father—the Spirit of truth who proceeds from the Father—he will testify about me. You also will testify, because you have been with me from the beginning" (John 15:26–27).

Without the presence of the Spirit in their lives, the disciples were unprepared to face the persecution that was to come their way as followers of Jesus Christ. It was the Spirit that would "teach [them] all things and remind [the disciples] of everything [Jesus had] told [them]" (John 14:26). Only the Spirit had the power to "convict the world of sin and of righteousness and of judgment" (John 16:8–10) and not the persuasive arguments of humans. The day of Pentecost would have never happened if the Holy Spirit had not come down "like that of a violent rushing wind" and rested upon them "like flames of fire" enabling them to "speak in different tongues" and share the message of the gospel in the native languages of the multitude gathered for the festival.[312] Despite three years of following the Master, the disciples were unprepared to fulfill the task he had given them. They needed the power of the Holy Spirit to come upon each of them. That is why Jesus said, "It is to your advantage that I go away; for if I do not go away, the Helper will not come to you; but if I depart, I will send Him to you" (John 16:7 NKJV).

The same is true today. We also need the presence of the Holy Spirit in our lives. The apostle Paul assures us:

> You, however, are not in the flesh, but in the Spirit,
> if indeed the Spirit of God lives in you. If anyone

does not have the Spirit of Christ, he does not belong to him. Now if Christ is in you, the body is dead because of sin, but the Spirit gives life because of righteousness. And if the Spirit of him who raised Jesus from the dead lives in you, then he who raised Christ from the dead will also bring your mortal bodies to life through his Spirit who lives in you (Romans 8:9–11).

Notice the passage says several times: "if ... the Spirit of God lives in you; ... if Christ is in you ...; if the Spirit ... lives in you; ... through his Spirit who lives in you." It is the presence of the Spirit in the life of the one who follows Jesus that gives us life beyond anything we have ever experienced before.

From the moment we believe in Jesus, confessing our belief in him and our willingness to follow him, the Spirit indwells us, and we become the temple of the Holy Spirit.[313] As his followers, Christ has "sealed us and gave us the Spirit in our hearts as a pledge" (2 Corinthians 1:22 NASB), guaranteeing our inheritance in his presence forever and ever. The Lord promised that "the Spirit of truth ... will testify about me" and "when he comes, he will guide you into all truth" (John 15:26, 16:13). Moments before his ascension into heaven, Jesus said to his followers, "You shall receive power when the Holy Spirit has come upon you; and you shall be witnesses to Me in Jerusalem, and in all Judea and Samaria, and to the end of the earth" (Acts 1:8 NKJV). Just as Jesus was able to encourage, guide, and help the disciples when he was present on earth, today the Spirit still encourages, guides, and helps his followers. It is by the power of the Holy Spirit that we bear fruit and glorify our Savior and Lord, especially in the most tragic and trying of circumstances. Through the Spirit, the Father's redemptive work is no longer limited by the physical restraints of the human body, but he empowers Christians around the world at the same time to fulfill the Great Commission. The Beloved Apostle John reminded us, "By this we know that we abide in him and he in us, because he has given us of his Spirit" (1 John 4:13 ESV).

Furthermore, the disciples could not follow him because **they still had much to learn about Jesus and from him.** Consider with me for a moment what Jesus did during the forty days following his resurrection until his ascension into heaven. Now remember, at first the disciples were engaged in a desperate struggle to understand and accept the resurrection, although they had seen him raise three other people.[314] "Yes, the tomb was empty, but was the Lord really alive?—as the women claimed," they must have wondered. And, yes, the Lord had appeared to Simon Peter.[315] But their response was somewhat guarded because they were struggling just to grasp his resurrection. For this reason, as he appeared to the two men on the road to Emmaus, Jesus said unto them,

> "How foolish and slow you are to believe all that the prophets have spoken! Wasn't it necessary for the Messiah to suffer these things and enter into his glory?" Then beginning with Moses and all the Prophets, he interpreted for them the things concerning himself in all the Scriptures. (Luke 24:25–27)

Walking along the road to Emmaus, the Lord pointed them to the Old Testament scripture regarding his life, crucifixion, and resurrection, so they might understand what had occurred as he died and arose from the grave. His aim was that they might be able to declare the meaning of the gospel to other people equally confused and walking in unbelief. It was not until later that evening as he led them in prayer that Jesus revealed himself unto them. Hours later as he appeared to his followers in the upper room, he first set their troubled hearts and souls at ease by showing them his nail-pierced hands and where the spear had been thrust into his side. Then the

Lord began to open "their minds to understand the Scriptures" so they might proclaim "repentance for forgiveness of sin (W. C. Kaiser 2004)… to all the nations" (Luke 24:36–49). A few days later, as he appeared unto seven of his disciples who returned to fishing, he sought to restore Peter after his denial and encourage each man as he prepared them for the future.[316] The disciples were not prepared for the task that was before them. They needed this additional time of study and interaction with the Master Teacher.

Are we any different? Do we know the scriptures as well as we should? The answer is more than likely—no, we don't. We need to read God's Word more, not only to know more facts, but to understand God's great desire and purpose for his children. Just as it is impossible to really know someone without spending time with them, we cannot know God without reading and studying his Word and spending time in prayer talking with him; therefore, Bible reading and prayer must become a daily part of your lives if we are to grow in our relationship with Jesus Christ. I believe this is the one action every Christian can take that will transform our lives more than anything else. If we read his Word and spend time in daily prayer, the Holy Spirit will open the Bible to our understanding. And as our understanding of the Father's desire for us grows, in turn we will live closer to him, bearing fruit and glorifying his Holy Name.

Moreover, **the disciples did not totally believe in Jesus**. It goes without saying, for all of us, that we usually struggle to follow someone we did not fully believe in. This is true of soldiers and their sergeant; athletes following their coach; people following a politician or some other leader. It was true in the day of the Lord's earthly ministry. As the events of the night reveal, the disciples still had their questions. This was obvious as Jesus challenged their declaration that they believed that he was from God, saying, "Now you believe. The time is coming, and is already here, when all of you will be scattered. Each of you will go your own way and leave me all alone. Yet, I'm not all alone, because the Father is with me" (John

16:31–32 GW). Their doubts about him still played across their minds and those doubts kept them from surrendering themselves completely to him.

Earlier in the upper room, the Lord Jesus Christ had challenged his disciples. "Believe me that I am in the Father and the Father is in me. Otherwise believe because of the works themselves" (John 14:11). Regardless what they had said, the disciples still had their doubts about Jesus. They were struggling to believe the words he was sharing with them, and the Master's works were the only real proof they had that he was who he claimed to be. Just as the disciples later found it difficult to believe that Jesus arose from the dead, it is even more difficult for people to believe in him today. For various reasons, many stubbornly refuse to believe in him. Belief in Jesus can be so arduous that Jesus said to Thomas as he appeared to the disciples for a second time in the upper room, "Have you believed because you have seen me? Blessed are those who have not seen and yet have believed" (John 20:29 ESV).

Look first at his family. They had known him all their lives, and yet they struggled to believe he was the promised Messiah. I would think they had heard something of his birth. They lived with him, so they knew him better than anyone, yet scripture says, "not even his brothers believed in him" (John 7:5). Although his mother, Mary, and brothers often followed him, it was not until after his resurrection that his brothers James and Judas are listed among his followers.[317]

Even the people in his hometown of Nazareth refused to believe in him and attempted "to throw him over a cliff" (Luke 4:16–30). Perhaps it was because they knew him so well that they struggled to believe in him. After all, it is likely that some of them had run through the streets playing games with him when they were children. As adults, others had paid him to do carpentry work for them. They had seen him sweat in his daily labors. Perhaps over a shared meal they had talked of life, politics, and God. Maybe being familiar with Jesus made belief difficult. What about you? Do you struggle to accept and believe that Jesus came to be the Savior of the world?

Also, we must not forget that although Judas walked with him for three years, he never surrendered himself to Jesus. He always held something back and never committed himself fully to the Master. Evidently, he believed more in money than he believed in Jesus. In the end he conspired with the religious leaders and betrayed him for thirty pieces of silver. And when he came to his senses, it was too late. Jesus was already on his way to the cross; so rather than confess his sin before God, Judas went out and hanged himself.[318] Do we believe more in money than in Jesus?

Likewise, the religious leaders simply refused to believe that Jesus was the Messiah they had sought for so many years. They knew the promises of God as proclaimed by the prophets, yet they failed to see the fulfillment of prophecy in Jesus. He simply did not meet their lofty ideals of what the Messiah should be. Time after time Jesus lovingly sought to convince them, but at some point it became obvious that they would never acknowledge him as the Son of God. The power and position they held within the nation of Israel were more important to them than the truth of holy scripture. Their pride demanded that these be protected at all cost. It was just not in their self-interest to believe in Jesus. So instead they sought to destroy him, and in the end, they cried out without remorse for his crucifixion and mocked him as he died. Then they further rejected the proclamation of his death and resurrection and sought to destroy the growing church by killing his followers. Is pride keeping you from surrendering to the Lord's tender call? Does your own self-interest keep you from surrendering completely to Jesus Christ?

Earlier in his ministry, the religious leaders were right on target when they recognized that only God has forgiven sin, but they refused to believe that Jesus was the Messiah come from God.[319] Instead, the religious leaders mocked him and began to seek ways to kill Him. Never one to back down to opposition, Jesus responded by condemning them.

> You are from below, ... I am from above. You are
> of this world; I am not of this world. Therefore, I
> told you that you will die in your sins. For if you do
> not believe that I am he you will die in your sins.
> (John 8:23–24)

As the Savior's words indicate, **failure to believe in Jesus is extremely dangerous.** The sad fact is that failure to believe in Jesus will cost us everything—even our eternal soul. Instead of yielding to unbelief, we need to become like the man who came first to the disciples asking them to cast out a demon from his son. And when they could not heal him, they brought the boy to the Master. After learning more about the situation, Jesus said to him, "Everything is possible for the one who believes." And we are told that immediately the father of the young boy cried out, 'I believe; help my unbelief'" (Mark 9:14–24). Likewise, we need help in our unbelief because belief is sometimes so very difficult, even for the most dedicated follower of Jesus. That help comes through the Holy Spirit, which indwells every true follower of Jesus Christ.

As we see so often throughout scripture, unbelief can keep us from following Jesus. It can take our focus from Jesus to our circumstances. Unbelief can lead us to the wrong conclusions, as well as disobedience and total rebellion against God. If left uncheck, unbelief will steer us so far away from God that we no longer can hear his Spirit speak to us above all the noise of life. Unbelief is dangerous—for the Christian, as well as the non-Christian. So how do we recover from unbelief?

For the follower of Jesus, a simple method of recovery can be found in the Savior's words to the church at Ephesus. Confronting their waywardness, Jesus say, "I have this against you, that you have abandoned the love you had at first. Remember therefore from where you have fallen; repent, and do the works you did at first. If not, I will come to you and remove your lampstand from its place, unless you repent" (Revelation 2:4–5 ESV). The source of the risen

Lord's displeasure can most likely be found in the false doctrine Paul charged his young apprentice Timothy to faithfully oppose.[320] But apparently by the time John received the Revelation half a century later, the problem with false doctrine had become so great that it had essentially taken over the church. The people had so deluded the gospel with falsehood that very few true followers could be found. Is the same thing happening in the church today? Are false teachers and their erroneous doctrines destroying the church from within? I am fearful that such is the case.

If so, the risen Lord's words apply to us as well. His challenge to the church at Ephesus could be summed up in three words: Remember! Repent! Return! As children of God, we must remember where we were when we first came to Jesus—his unconditional love for us and the love we once had for him. We must remember our desire to know and obey him in all things. We need to honor him by maintaining the purity of our teaching, while holding fast to his Word. Second, we must confess and repent of the sin that has drawn us away from the Lord Jesus Christ. Finally, we must once again return and earnestly seek his face through Bible study, prayer, and the godly service that had once brought us such joy in the Lord. Nothing else will restore our love for the Master of heaven and earth. Will you once again become a sold-out follower of Jesus?

For the nonbeliever the path is very similar. First, we must come to Jesus admitting we are sinners and our need for a Savior. Second, the non-Christian must accept the facts of the gospel and believe in Jesus as the Savior of the world sent by a loving God. Third, we must confess our sin, turn from our evil ways, and place our focus upon Jesus, who loved us enough to die for us. As we do this, God does a whole host of wonderful things in our lives. Our sins are forgiven, and we are washed completely clean by the blood Jesus shed on the cross. We are transformed by the power of the Spirit into a member of the family of God and a child of the King, which also means we receive eternal life. At the same time, the Holy Spirit, God's Holy presence, takes up residence in our lives to help us live for him. And these are just to name a few things that occur at the moment of our salvation.

The point is that **God wants to have an eternal relationship with each one of us.** Through his grace and mercy, he has done everything possible to make that happen, but we must come and receive his gift of salvation. Every day he lovingly reaches out to us, but we must stop running frantically around and listen to his voice as he speaks to us through his Word the Bible, through prayer, his Spirit, the encouragement of another believer, circumstances, or in other ways. Only as we do this will our relationship with God the Father grow and mature. Just as with any friend, only as we spend time with him can we enjoy the many blessings that come by knowing him personally.

My friend, do you believe in Jesus? Will you come right now to Jesus and receive him as your personal Savior? My fellow believer, will you return to your first love and once again seek to follow Jesus every day? Regardless of who you are, he is waiting for you.

Food for Thought

Who do you believe Jesus is? Why?

How does what you believe about Jesus affect the way you follow him?

What in your life keeps you from completely following Jesus?

He asked him the third time, "Simon, son of John, do you love me?"

Peter was grieved that he asked him the third time, "Do you love me??" He said, "Lord, you know everything; you know that I love you."

"Truly I tell you, when you were younger, you would tie your belt and walk wherever you wanted. But when you grow old, you will stretch out your hands and someone else will tie you and carry you where you don't want to go." He said this to indicate by what kind of death Peter would glorify God.

After saying this, he told him, "Follow me."

So Peter turned around and saw the disciple Jesus loved following them, the one who had leaned back against Jesus at the supper and asked, "Lord, who is the one that's going to betray you?" When Peter saw him, he said to Jesus, "Lord, what about him??"

"If I want him to remain until I come," Jesus answered, "what is that to you? As for you, follow me." (John 21:17–22)

One Last Challenge

As we come to the end of this book, I have found myself thinking about the third time the risen Lord appeared to his disciples along the seashore of the Sea of Galilee, otherwise known as the Sea of Tiberias. For some unexplained reason, seven of the disciples had decided to go fishing once again. Perhaps they went just because they missed fishing. After all, to the best of our knowledge it had been some time since they had been involved in their chosen profession. They were still in their boat on the water after a fishless night when Jesus appeared and instructed them to cast their nets on the right side of the boat—resulting in a catch of 153 fish. Enlightened by the enormous catch, John recognized Jesus and cried out to Peter, "It is the Lord" (John 21:1–16). In response Peter jumped overboard and swim ashore. Moreover, scripture tells us that all through the meal Jesus had prepared for them, the disciples did not question who he was; "they knew it was the Lord" (John 21:12).

Much has been written about the conversation between Jesus and Peter that followed the meal as Jesus repeatedly asked him the question, "Simon Peter, do you love?" The deep spiritual meaning of the different Greek words used by Peter and the Lord for the word *love* have been explained far better by others than I ever could. After each response by Peter, the Good Shepherd offered him a challenge: "Feed my lambs ... Shepherd my sheep ... Feed my sheep" (John 21:15–17). The simple truth is that although Peter had denied knowing him in the strongest of terms, the Master was not finished with Peter. There was still work to be done for the kingdom of God. By the power of the Holy Spirit, Peter would actually live up to the name Jesus gave him and become The Rock.[321] Accepting the Lord's call, he will "strengthen [his] brothers" (Luke 22:32) during the coming days of persecution as they share the message of the gospel throughout the Roman world.[322] But for now, in frustration and despair, Peter answered the last question: "Lord, you know everything; you know that I love you." Yes, the Lord Jesus Christ knew everything. He knew the depth of Peter's love for him. He also knew how Peter's life would end as he added a word of prophecy regarding his future death. As an old man, Peter was to follow Jesus in death just as he had boasted in the upper room.[323]

Finally, the Lord added the command, "Follow me" (John 21:18–19).

The sense of hopeless felt by Peter as he answered the Lord's final question has always struck a sickening discord within my heart. How much do I love Jesus? Am I willing to sacrifice everything for him? If necessary, how would I face suffering and persecution for his name's sake? Am I willing to follow the Master even if it meant dying for him? How about you? Does it turn your stomach to consider the possibility that you may not be as committed to Jesus as you claim? That you may not love him as much as you have tried to make others believe?

Hearing the Lord's prediction, Peter pointed to John, who was following them, and asked, "Lord, what about him?" To which Jesus answered, "If I want him to remain until I come, what is that to you? As for you, follow me" (John 21:20–22).

In my mind's eye, I can almost see Jesus and Peter standing face to face. Lovingly looking into his eyes, the Lord places one hand on Peter's shoulder, while pressing the fingers of his other hand against his chest, saying, "Peter, the plans I have for John are none of your business." Then slowly and gently striking his chest to emphasis each word. "You! Follow! Me!"

The truth of his words is inescapable. As the Lord's command to Peter indicates, following Jesus is a call to personal commitment. No one can make such a commitment for you. Each one of us must decide for ourselves if we will follow him or not. It really does not matter what others do or what happens to them. All that truly matters is the nature of the commitment we make to him. This has been our emphasis throughout this book. If you claim to be a Christian, you are to just follow Jesus. There is no other option. There can be no compromise or half-heartedness. There can be no wandering back to the ways of the world whenever it appeals to us or when things get difficult. As we have seen time after time, if we are to be obedient unto him, we must—not should or ought too— we must diligently seek to follow Jesus ever moment of every day through everything that happens in our everyday lives. And when we fail, we must immediately come before him in sincere confession and repentance, so he might restore our relationship with him. We must never forget that Jesus said, "Blessed ... are those who hear the word of God, and obey it" (Luke 11:28 NIV).

Brothers and sisters, are you following Jesus with all that is in you? If not, why not come to him right now? Don't put it off until later. Surrender everything to him—your life, your all.

Although the divine promise found in the book of Jeremiah was originally meant for the rebellious Jewish nation, they still hold great meaning for all believers throughout all times, especially in the sinful days in which we live. As we surrender our lives completely unto him, we can rest assured that God loves us, and even in the most difficult of circumstances he is at work all around us.

> For I know the plans I have for you
> —this is the LORD's declaration—
> plans for your well-being, not for disaster,
> to give you a future and a hope.
> You will call to me and come and pray to me,
> and I will listen to you.

You will seek me and find me
when you search for me with all your heart.
(Jeremiah 29:11–13)

My friend, God has a plan for your life. The only way you can fulfill that plan is to totally surrender your life unto him. Will you do so right now in the quietness of this moment? He is waiting with open arms for you.

About the Author

Billy and Susan Stines in Armenia

After serving for nearly forty years in six churches scattered around North and South Carolina, Billy J. Stines retired in a formal sense from the gospel ministry on December 31, 2017. In retirement he is still active in the local church, the association, and state convention, as well as participating in mission trips. Throughout the years, his greatest support and encouragement has come from Susan, his loving wife of nearly forty-two years. Together they are very proud of their two married sons, their daughters-in-law, and four grandchildren—two boys and two girls. All four are under four. As you may guess, they try to spend as much time as possible with their family. Although he has written several dramas and created musicals for the local church, this is Billy's first attempt at writing a book. The Lord willing, there will be others in the future.

Endnotes

1 Matthew 13:1–9, 18–23.
2 John 15:8.
3 Matthew 22:37–40; Mark 12:29–31.

Chapter 1: The Call of the Disciples

4 Anthony T. Evans, *Tony Evans' Book of Illustrations: Stories, Quotes, and Anecdotes from More than 30 Years of Preaching and Public Speaking*, © 2009 (Database © 2009 WORD*search*), "Commitment," "Spiritual Maturity."
5 Matthew 4:18–22, 9:9.
6 Luke 5:5.
7 Matthew 4:13, 9:1.
8 Genesis 17:3–5.
9 Genesis 50:19–20.
10 Exodus 3:1.
11 1 Samuel 3:3–10.
12 1 Samuel 16:11.
13 1 Kings 19:19.
14 Isaiah 6:1–13.
15 Amos 1:1.
16 Luke 1:27; Matthew 1:25.
17 Acts 9:1–18.
18 John 1:35–42.
19 Bruce B. Barton, Mark Fackler, Linda K. Taylor, and David R. Veerman; contributing editors: James C. Galvin, EdD, and Ronald A. Beers. *Life Application Bible Commentary: Matthew.* (Database © 2014 WORD*search*).

20   John 6:44.

21   Matthew 6:21, 10:32–33; Luke 12:8–-9.

22   Matthew 13:1–9, 18–23.

23   Matthew 7:24–27.

24   2 Corinthians 5:17.

25   Romans 6:12.

26   Matthew 8:14–15.

27   Michael J. Wilkins, *The NIV Application Commentary: Matthew* (© 2004, database © 2013 WORD*search*).

28   R. C. H. Lenski, *Lenski New Testament Commentary: Matthew: Commentary on the New Testament*, vols. 1–12, (Augsburg, 1961, database © 2008 WORD*search*).

29   Matthew 9:19–22.

30   John 21:1–3.

31   John MacArthur Jr., *The MacArthur New Testament Commentary: Matthew 1–7.* (© 1985 by Moody Bible Institute of Chicago, all rights reserved, database © 2015 WORD*search*).

32   Matthew 6:24.

33   Michael P. Green, ed., *Illustrations for Biblical Preaching* (Chicago: Moody Bible Institute, 1985, all rights reserved, database © 2008 WORD*search*).

34   Luke 5:1–11.

35   Matthew 4:19; Mark 1:17.

36   Matthew 14:21, 16:6, 17:20.

37   Luke 9:1–6, 10, 10:1–3, 17.

38   Acts 2.

39   Luke 9:1–6, 10:1–24.

40   Acts 2:47, 5:14.

41   Stuart Webert and Max Anders, *Holman New Testament Commentary: Matthew.* (Broadman & Holman, Nashville, TN, 2000, database © 2005 WORD*search*).

42   Greg S. Keener, *The IVP New Testament Commentary Series: Matthew* (© 1997, database © 2006 WORD*search*).

43   Romans 16:1; 2 Corinthians 6:4.

44   James Orr, MA, DD, general editor, *The International Standard Bible Encyclopaedia* (Howard-Severance, 1915, database © 2014 WORD*search*).

45   *Tony Evans' Book of Illustrations*, "Victory," "Overcome."

46   B. B. McKinney, "Let Others See Jesus in You," *Baptist Hymnal.* (Nashville, TN: Convention Press, 1991), 571.

Chapter 2: The Call to the Cross

47   John 2:19.
48   John 3:14; Numbers 21:6–9.
49   Matthew 12:38–40, 16:4.
50   Matthew 16:34–37.
51   John 4:10–14.
52   John 6:48–58.
53   Psalm 51.
54   John 5:16–17.
55   Romans 6:15–18; 2 Peter 2:18–19.
56   Matthew 4:1–11.
57   1 John 1:9.
58   Marin Nystrom, "As the Deer," (Maranatha Praise Administered, 1984, by Copyright Company, Nashville, TN).
59   1 Peter 4:16.
60   Clifton J. Allen, *Broadman Bible Commentary: Matthew-Mark* (Broadman Press, 1969, database © 2017 WORD*search*).
61   Acts 3–5.
62   Acts 6–7.
63   Acts 12:1–2.
64   Acts 8:1.
65   Acts 16.
66   Warren W. Wiersbe, *Bible Exposition Commentary* (BE Series): New Testament—vol. 1 (© 2001, database © 2007 WORD*search*).
67   R. Kent Hughes, *Preaching the Word: Luke*, vol. 2, "That You May Know the Truth" (copyright 1998, database © 2008 WORD*search*).
68   John 14:21, 23–24, 15:10, 14.
69   John 3:16.
70   1 Peter 2:21.
71   John 15:14.
72   Ephesians 4:32–5:2.
73   Matthew 10:38, 16:4; Mark 8:34; Luke 14:27; John 12:25.
74   Revelation 21:1ff.
75   Luke 9:25.
76   Matthew 10:52–53.
77   John G. Butler, *Analytical Bible Expositor: Luke* (© 2008, database © 2013 WORD*search*).

78 William Hendriksen, *Baker New Testament Commentary: Exposition of the Gospel according to Luke* (© 1978, database © 2008 WORD*search*).

79 Matthew 6:2, 5, 16.

80 John 19:38–40.

81 Leviticus 21:11; Numbers 5:2–3, 9:6.

82 Thoralf Gilbrant and Tor Inge Gilbrant, *The Complete Biblical Library Commentary: Luke* (World copyright © 1986, database © 2009 WORD*search*).

83 John Phillips, *The John Phillips Commentary Series: Exploring the Gospel of Luke*. (Database © 2009 WORD*search*).

84 Matthew 26:57–58, 69–75.

85 Luke 12:8–9.

86 Luke 22:60–62.

87 1 Corinthians 1:23.

88 Romans 2:5.

89 Leviticus 11:44–45; 1 Peter 1:15–16.

90 Ezekiel 18:4; Romans 6:23.

91 2 Corinthians 5:21.

92 Titus 2:14.

93 Romans 5:6–9.

94 Galatians 3:26.

95 Romans 10:9–13.

96 Romans 8:23.

97 Mal Couch and Ed Hindson, *Twenty-First Century Biblical Commentary Series: The Gospel of Luke: Christ, the Son of Man*. (© 2006 by Tyndale Theological Seminary, database © 2010 WORD*search*).

98 Romans 3:10–12, 23.

99 *Twenty-First Century Biblical Commentary Series: The Gospel of Luke: Christ, the Son of Man.*

100 *Leadership*, vol. 10, no. 4., *Today's Best Illustrations*—vols. 1–4., complied by Elesha Hodge (© 1997 by Christianity Today, database © 2012 WORD*search*), "Better Than Instructions."

Chapter 3: The Call to Relinquish

101 *Tony Evans' Book of Illustrations: Stories, Quotes, and Anecdotes*, "Commitment." "Sacrifice," "Giving," "Concept of Surrender."

102 Luke 9:52–62; Matthew 8:19–22.

[103] *750 Engaging Illustrations*, Craig Brian Larson and Leadership Journal (© 1993 by Christianity Today); Craig Brian Larson, *Contemporary Illustrations for Preachers, Teachers, and Writers* (© 1996); Craig Brian Larson, *Choice Contemporary Stories and Illustrations* (© 1998, database © 2008 WORD*search*).

[104] Matthew 8:19.

[105] John 2:23–25.

[106] John 5:18.

[107] John 6:66.

[108] Matthew 8:34.

[109] Luke 9:53.

[110] William Barclay, *Barclay's Daily Study Bible* (NT) (Database © 2008 WORD*search*).

[111] Luke 21:1–4.

[112] Acts 2:42–47, 4:34–37.

[113] Acts 4:1–37, 5:42, 7:54–60.

[114] Barclay's Daily Study (NT).

[115] *Baker New Testament Commentary: Exposition of the Gospel According to Luke.*

[116] Exodus 20:12.

[117] Matthew 15:3–6.

[118] Analytical Bible Expositor: Luke.

[119] John MacArthur Jr., *The MacArthur New Testament Commentary: Luke 6–10* (© 2011 by John MacArthur, database © 2014 WORD*search*).

[120] *Word Bible Commentary: Luke,* (© Galaxie Software, database © 2009 WORD*search*).

[121] Philip W. Comfort, *Cornerstone Biblical Commentary,* vol. 12: *Luke and Acts* (*Luke* © 2006 by Allison A. Trites, *Acts* copyright © 2006 by William J. Larkin, database © 2008 WORD*search*).

[122] Genesis 22:1–19.

[123] Matthew 6:1–18.

[124] *750 Engaging Illustrations*, #586, "Sacrifice."

[125] Luke 19:10.

[126] 1 Kings 19:19–21.

[127] Genesis 19:17–20.

[128] *Preaching the Word: Luke,* vol. 1, "That You May Know the Truth."

[129] Revelation 19:11.

[130] Revelation 20:11–15.

[131] *750 Engaging Illustrations*, #83, "Commitment."

[132] *750 Engaging Illustrations*, #393, "Love."

[133] Galatians 2:20.

[134] *The Good Life*, A musical by John Peterson, "Christ Lives in Me," S.A.T.B. © 1972 by Singspiration.

Chapter 4: The Call to Count the Cost

[135] Luke 14:15–24.

[136] *Tony Evans's Book of Illustrations*, Commitment," "Spiritual Life," "Manifestation of Blessings."

[137] Jon Courson, *Jon Courson's Application Commentary: New Testament* (© 2003, database © 2013 WORD*search*).

[138] *Complete Biblical Library Commentary: Luke.*

[139] Walter C. Kaiser Jr., Peter H. Davids, F. F. Bruce, and Manfred T. Brauch, *Hard Sayings of the Bible* (InterVarsity Press, 1996, all rights reserved, database © 2004 WORD*search*).

[140] *Preaching the Word: Luke*, vol. 11, "That You May Know the Truth."

[141] *Preaching the Word: Luke*, vol. 11, "That You May Know the Truth."

[142] John 3:16.

[143] Romans 5:8.

[144] 2 Corinthians 5:21.

[145] 2 Corinthians 4:14–17.

[146] Romans 4:25, 5:1.

[147] Romans 4:23–26.

[148] 1 Corinthians 6:20.

[149] Genesis 3.

[150] Romans 6:23.

[151] Romans 8:38–39.

[152] Matthew 10:30.

[153] John W. Cox, ed., *The Minsters Manual* (San Francisco: Harper & Row, 1984), 302; *Notable Harbour Illustrations*—vol. 10: *Illustrations* (reprint from vol. 20, *Brian's Lines* 2004) (Database © 2004 WORD*search*), "Commitment."

[154] James Burton Coffman *Coffman Commentaries: Commentary on Luke* (© 1984 ACU Press, database © 2017 WORD*search*).

[155] Romans 5:8.

[156] *The Bible Exposition Commentary* (Be Series): *New Testament*, vol. 1.

[157] *Jon Courson's Application Commentary New Testament.*

158 *The Bible Exposition Commentary* (Be Series): New Testament, vol. 1.

159 John 12:23–28.

160 *Illustrations for Biblical Preaching*, "Commitment."

161 Numbers 13–14.

162 Deuteronomy 1:22–23.

163 Numbers 13:25–33.

164 Exodus 23:20–32.

165 Numbers 14:1–4.

166 Genesis 7–9.

167 Genesis 2:5.

168 Genesis 12:1–4.

169 Genesis 13.

170 Books of Exodus, Numbers, Leviticus and Deuteronomy.

171 Book of Joshua.

172 Daniel 3.

173 Daniel 6.

174 Acts 21:37, 23:10, 24:10–21, 26:1–32.

175 Darrell L. Bock, *The NIV Application Commentary: Luke.* (© 1996, database © 2013 WORD*search*).

176 *The NIV Application Commentary: Luke.*

177 Paul Powell, *Jump Starting Dead Churches* (Dallas: SBC Annuity Board, 1995), 12–13; *Notable Harbour Illustrations*—vol. 7. Reprint from vol. 17, 2001. (Database © 2013 WORD*search*).

178 James S. Hewett, *Illustrations Unlimited* (© 1988, database © 2005 WORD*search*), "Sacrifice," "Surrender to Christ."

179 *Baptist Hymnal.* "Trust and Obey.," Words by John H. Sammis. Music by Daniel B. Towner. (Nashville, TN: Convention Press, 1991), 447.

180 John Phillips, *The John Phillips Commentary Series: Exploring the Gospel of Luke* (Database © 2009 WORD*search*).

181 John 11:42.

182 1 Samuel 17.

183 1 Kings 18:20–40.

184 2 Chronicles 20:1–30.

185 Matthew 1:18–25; Luke 1:26–38.

186 *Illustrations Unlimited*, "Sacrifice," 4, "The High Cost of Making Peace."

187 *The Expositor's Bible Commentary: Matthew, Mark, Luke*, vol. 8 (© 1984 by Zondervan, database © 2014 WORD*search*).

188 *The Expositor's Bible Commentary: Matthew, Mark, Luke*, vol. 8.

189 *The Complete Biblical Library Commentary: Luke.*

190 *Barclay's Daily Study Bible* (NT).

191 Matthew 6:24.

192 "Pastor Tim's Clean Laugh List," submitted by Mark Morning, managing editor of *Campus Life—More Perfect Illustrations: For Every Topic and Occasion*, Craig Brian Larson. (© Tyndale House, Copyright 2003 by Christianity Today International, all rights reserved, database © 2008 WORD*search*), "Commitment," "Me," and "Work."

Chapter 5: The Call to Obedience

193 Associated Press, "Student Collects Fake Parking Fines," Sept. 15, 2004, submitted by Jim Sandell; John Wilson, *More Fresh Illustrations* (Database © 2007 WORD*search*), "Money."

194 Mark 10:17–22.

195 Mark 10:32.

196 R. Kent Hughes, *Preaching the Word: Mark*, vol. 11 (© 1989, database © 2008 WORD*search*).

197 David Platt, *Counter Culture: Following Christ in an Anti-Christian Age* (© Tyndale Momentum, revised 2017. Ebook), 55.

198 Dietrich Bonhoeffer, *The Cost of Discipleship*. (New York: Touchstone, ebook) 69.

199 Coffman, James Burton, *Coffman Commentaries: Commentary on Mark* (© 1975, ACU Press, database © 2017 WORD*search*).

200 William Hendriksen, *Baker New Testament Commentary: Exposition of the Gospel According to Mark* (© 1975, database © 2008 WORD*search*).

201 *Baker New Testament Commentary: Exposition of the Gospel According to Mark.*

202 *Bible Exposition Commentary* (Be Series): New Testament, vol. 1.

203 David E. Garland, *The NIV Application Commentary: Mark* (© 1996, database © 2013 WORD*search*).

204 James McGowan, *Twenty-First Century Biblical Commentary Series: The Gospel of Mark* (© 2006 by Scofield Ministries, database © 2010 WORD*search*).

205 R. C. H. Lenski, *Lenski New Testament Commentary: The Interpretation of St. Mark's Gospel, Commentary on the New Testament*, vols. 1–12 (Augsburg Publishing, 1961, database © 2008 WORD*search*).

206 Luke 23:39–43.

207 John 5:18; 7:1, 30–32; 8:59; 10:30–33; 11:45–57.

208 2 Corinthians 5:19–21; 1 Peter 2:24.

209 John 1:12–13.

210 Hebrews 12:2.

211 Luke 15:7, 19, 22–24.

212 Acts 16:19–31.

213 *Life Application Bible Commentary: Mark*. © 1994 by Livingstone Corp. All rights reserved. Published by Tyndale House, Wheaton, IL. Contributing editors: James C. Galvin, EdD, and Ronald A. Beers. Life Application is a registered trademark of Tyndale House. Scripture quotations marked NIV are taken from the Holy Bible, New International Version. (Database © 2014 WORD*search*).

214 *Life Application Bible Commentary: Mark*.

215 John G. Butler, *Analytical Bible Expositor: Mark* (© 2008, database © 2013 WORD*search*).

216 Matthew 6:19–21.

217 1 Corinthians 6:19–20; 2 Corinthians 6:16.

218 1 Corinthians 4:5.

219 Matthew 10:32–33.

220 John 1:12.

221 Elisabeth Elliot, *Shadow of the Almighty* (New York: Harper & Row, 1979), 247; John MacArthur, *MacArthur New Testament Commentary: Mark 9–16* (Database © 2015 WORD*search*).

222 Matthew 20:1; Luke 13:30.

223 *Barclay's Daily Study Bible* (NT).

224 Matthew 21:1–4.

225 John 13:14–15.

226 http://www.detnews.com (*Detroit News*), "Women Meet at Christian retreat, Agree on Kidney donation," September 22, 2004, submitted by Jim Sandell, *More Fresh Illustrations*, "Sacrifice."

Chapter 6: The Call to Service

227 John 12:20–22.

228 John 1:44.

229 John 1:45.

230 John G. Butler, *Analytical Bible Expositor: John* (© 2009, database © 2013 WORD*search*).

231 William Hendriksen, *Baker New Testament Commentary: Exposition of the Gospel According to John* (1953, Database © 2008 WORD*search*).

232 Luke 18:15–17.

233 John 1:40–42.

234 John 6:9.

235 Acts 1:8; Matthew 28:19–20.

236 John 2:4; 4:21, 23; 7:38; 8:20.

237 John 12:12–19; Matthew 21:1–9; Mark 11:1–10; Luke 19:29–38.

238 Genesis 3:15.

239 Matthew 2:16.

240 Luke 4:16–20.

241 Matthew 16:21, 17:22–23, 20:18–19.

242 John 11:53–57.

243 John 12:5–6.

244 R. C. H. Lenski, *Lenski New Testament Commentary: John; Commentary on the New Testament*, vols. 1–12, (© 1961, Augsburg Publishing, database © 2008 WORD*search*).

245 Matthew 3:17, 17:5.

246 *Bible Exposition Commentary* (Be Series): New Testament, vol. 1.

247 Genesis 2:16–17, 3:19.

248 Romans 5:12–21.

249 Acts 9:1–22.

250 *Life Application Bible Commentary: John.* © 1993 by Livingstone. All rights reserved. Published by Tyndale House, Wheaton, IL. Editor: Philip Comfort, Ph.D. Contributing Editors: James C. Galvin, EdD, and Ronald A. Beers. Life Application is a registered trademark of Tyndale House. Scripture quotations marked NIV are taken from the Holy Bible, New International Version. (Database © 2014 WORD*search*).

251 Romans 12:1–2.

252 Psalm 102:3.

253 R. Kent Hughes, *Preaching the Word: John* (© 1999, database © 2008 WORD*search*).

254 *Illustrations for Biblical Preaching.* 152; Christian Life, Service in.

255 Matthew 4:10; John 4:23–24.

256 (Adapted from W. A. Criswell, *Acts* (Grand Rapids: Zondervan, 1983), 187–88.); *Illustrations for Biblical Preaching*, 1124, "Service, Priority of."

257 James 2:15–17.

258 John 1:29; 1 Peter 1:19.

259 Romans 6:18–22.

260   *CSB Study Bible* (Nashville, TN: Holman Bible Products, 2017); *Study Notes on Philippians* 2:9–11.

261   *Illustrations for Biblical Preaching*, 1222.

262   John 13:1–13.

263   Acts 2:4ff.

264   Acts 7:60.

265   Romans 8:11.

266   1 Corinthians 12:4–11.

267   Romans 8:16–17.

268   *Analytical Bible Expositor: John.*

269   Revelation 21:4.

270   *Illustrations for Biblical Preaching*, 1126, "Service, Rewards of."

Chapter 7: Why Can't I Follow You, Lord?

271   Roger L. Fredrikson, *The Preacher's Commentary: John* (© 1985 by Word Inc., database © 2015 WORD*search*).

272   John 14:15, 21, 23–24, 28; 15:10, 12–13, 17; 16:27; 17:23, 26.

273   *Broadman Bible Commentary: Luke-John.*

274   John 14:2, 18, 28; 16:5, 19, 28; 17:13.

275   John 7:33–36, 8:21–22.

276   Matthew 26:36–27:2; Mark 14:32–72; Luke 22:39–65; John 18:1–27.

277   John 11:45–57.

278   Matthew 27:11–2; Mark 15:1–20; Luke 22:66–71, 23:1–25; John 18:1–27.

279   Matthew 27:27–56; Mark 15:21–41; Luke 23:26–49; John 19:16–37.

280   Matthew 27:57–65; Mark 15:42–47; Luke 23:50–56; John 19:38–42.

281   Matthew 28:1–10; Mark 16:1–8; Luke 24:1–53; John 20:1-31, 21:1–25.

282   Acts 1:1–11.

283   John 14:1–3.

284   Hebrews 2:17–18.

285   Matthew 28:1–10; Mark 16:1–8; Luke 24, John 20.

286   Genesis 2:17, 3:19.

287   Genesis 7–9.

288   Genesis 11:1–9.

289   Romans 3:10–18.

290   Matthew 17:5; John 12:28.

291   See also 2 Corinthians 4:4.

292   *CSB Study Bible*, "Study Notes on Colossians 1:19–-20."
293   Leviticus 24:16.
294   Mark 14:63–64.
295   Luke 5:17–25.
296   Matthew 8:3, 13, 14–17; 19:6–7, 22, 25, 29–30.
297   Matthew 8:23–27, 14:22–33.
298   Matthew 8:28–34.
299   Luke 7:11–17; 8:49–56; John 11:1–44.
300   John 8:19.
301   Matthew 10:28–34.
302   Matthew 28:19–20; Mark 16:15; Acts 1:8.
303   *Illustrations for Biblical Preaching*, "Great Commission."
304   Jack Cottrell, PhD; Tony Ash, PhD; Beauford H. Bryant; Mark S. Krause, *The College Press NIV Commentary: John* (College Press, 1998, database © 2009 WORD*search*).
305   John Phillips, *The John Phillips Commentary Series: Exploring the Gospel of John* (© 1989, database © 2009 WORD*search*).
306   *Lenski New Testament: John.*
307   James Burton Coffman, *Coffman Commentaries: Commentary on John* (© 1984 ACU Press, database © 2017 WORD*search*).
308   Elmer Towns, Mal Couch and Ed Hindson, *Twenty-First Century Biblical Commentary Series: The Gospel of John* ® (2002 by Scofield Ministries, database © 2010 WORD*search*).
309   John 18:10–11.
310   John 13:38.
311   *Peaching the Word—John*: "That You May Believe."
312   Acts 2:2–4.
313   1 Corinthians 6:19–20.
314   Mark 5:36–43; Luke 7:11–17; John 11:35–44.
315   Luke 24:34; 1 Corinthians 15:5.
316   John 21.
317   Acts 1:14.
318   Matthew 27:5.
319   Matthew 9:1-8; Luke 5:18–36.
320   See 1 and 2 Timothy and Acts 20:20–38 regarding Paul's concerns about false teachers at the church at Ephesus.

One Last Challenge

321 John 1:42; Matthew 16:18.
322 Acts chapters 2–5, 10, 12:6–19; 1 Peter 3:13–17, 4:12–19.
323 John 13:37.

Biblical Resources

Allen, Clifton J. 2017. *Broadman Bible Commentary: Luke-John.* WORDsearch.

—. 2017. *Broadman Bible Commentary: Matthew-Mark.* WORDsearch.

Alpha-Imega Ministries. 2013. *Preacher's Outline and Sermon Bible—Commentary: Matthew.* WORDsearch.

Alpha-Omega Ministries. 2013. *Preacher's Outline and Sermon Bible—Commentary: John.* WORDsearch.

—. 2013. *Preacher's Outline and Sermon Bible—Commentary: Luke.* WORDsearch.

—. 2013. *Preacher's Outline and Sermon Bible—Commentary: Mark.* WORDsearch.

Augsburger, Myron S. and Lloyd J. Ogilvie. 2015. *The Preacher's Commentary: Matthew.* WORDsearch.

Barclay, William. 2008. *Barclay's Daily Study Bible (NT).* WORDsearch.

Barnes, Albert, and Robert Frew. 2014. *Barnes' Notes on the New Testament.* WORDsearch.

Barton, Bruce B., Mark Fackler, Linda K. Taylor, and David R. Veerman. 2014. *Life Application Bible Commentary: Matthew.* WORDsearch.

Belleville, Linda L. and Grant R. Osborne. 2006. *The IVP New Testament Commentary Series: 2 Corinthians.* WORDsearch.

Blomberg, Craig L. 2013. *New American Commentary: Matthew.* WORDsearch.

Bock, Darrell L. 2014. *The IVP New Testament Commentary Series: Luke.* WORDsearch.

—. 2013. *The NIV Application Commentary: Luke.* WORDsearch.

Boice., Linda. 2014. *Boice Expositional Commentary—Matthew, Volume 1.* WORDsearch.

Borchert, Gerald. 2013. *New American Commentary: John 12-21.* WORDsearch.

Brooks, James H. 2013. *New American Commentary: Mark.* WORDsearch.

Bulter, John G. 2013. *Analytical Bible Expositor: John.* WORDsearch.

—. 2013. *Analytical Bible Expositor: Luke.* WORDsearch.

—. 2013. *Analytical Bible Expositor: Mark.* WORDsearch.

Burge, Gary M. 2013. *The NIV Application Commentary: John.* WORDsearch.

Butler, John G. 2013. *Analytical Bible Expositor: Matthew.* WORDsearch.

Butler, Trent, and Max Anders. 2005. *Holman New Testament Commentary—Luke.* WORDsearch.

Carson, D. A. 2016. *Pillar New Testament Commentary: The Gospel According to John.* WORDsearch.

Charles, Price. 2011. *Focus on the Bible Commentary: Matthew.* WORDsearch.

Coffman, James Burton. 2017. *Coffman Commentaires: Commentary on Mark.* WORDsearch.

Coffman, James Burton. 2017. *Coffman Commentaires: Commentary on Luke.* WORDsearch.

—. 2017. *Coffman Commentaries: Commentary on John.* WORDsearch.

—. 2017. *Coffman Commentaries: Commentary on The Gospel of Matthew.* WORDsearch.

Comfort, Philip W., Allison Trites, and William J. Larkin. 2008. *Cornerstone Biblical Commentary: Volume 12: Luke and Acts.* WORDsearch.

Comfort, Philip W., David L. Turner, and Darrel L. Bock. 2008. *Cornerstone Biblical Commentary: Volume 11: Matthew and Mark.* WORDsearch.

Comfort, Philip W., Grant Osborne, and Philip W. & Hawley, Wendell C. Comfort. 2008. *Cornerstone Biblical Commentary: Volume 13: John and 1-3 John.* WORDsearch.

Cooper, Rodney, and Max Anders. 2015. *Holman New Testament Commentary—Mark.* WORDsearch.

Cottrell, Ph.D., Jack, Ph.D., Tony Ash, and Ph.D., Allen Black. 2009. *The College Press NIV Commentary: Matthew.* WORDsearch.

Cottrell, Ph.D., Jack, Ph.D., Tony Ash, Beauford H. Bryant, and Mark S. Krause. 2009. *The College Press NIV Commentary: John.* WORDsearch.

Cottrell, PhD, Jack, PhD, Tony Ash, and PhD, Allen Black. 2009. *The College Press NIV Commentary: Mark.* WORDsearch.

Cottrell, PhD, Jack, PhD, Tony Ash, and PhD, Allen. Black. 2009. *The College Press NIV Commentary: Luke.* WORDsearch.

Couch, Mall and Ed Hindson. 2010. *Twenty-First Century Biblical Commentary Series: The Gospel of Luke-Christ, the Son of Man.* WORDsearch.

Courson, Jon. 2013. *Jon Courson's Application Commentary: New Testament.* WORDsearch.

Edwards, James R. 2010. *Pillar New Testament Commentary: The Gospel According to Mark.* WORDsearch.

Excell, Spence. H. D. M. and Joseph S. 2008. *The Pulpit Commentary: Volume 15: Matthew.* WORDsearch.

Fredrikson, Roger L. 2015. *The Preacher's Commentary: John.* WORDsearch.

Galaxie Software. 2009. Word Bible *Bible Commentary - John.* WORDsearch.

—. 2009. Word *Bible Commentary - Luke.* WORDsearch.

—. 2009. Word *Bible Commentary - Mark*. WORDsearch.

—. 2009. Word *Bible Commentary - Matthew*. WORDsearch.

Gangel, Kenneth and Max Anders. 2005. *Holman New Testament Commentary—John*. WORDsearch.

Garland, David E. 2013. *The NIV Application Commentary: Mark*. WORDsearch.

Gilbrant., Thoralf Gilbrant and Tor Inge. 2009. *The Complete Biblical Library Commentary: John*. WORDsearch.

—. 2009. *The Complete Biblical Library Commentary: Luke*. WORDsearch.

—. 2009. *The Complete Biblical Library Commentary: Mark*. WORDsearch.

—. 2009. *The Complete Biblical Library Commentary: Matthew*. WORDsearch.

Grogan, Geoffrey W. 2011. *Focus on the Bible Commentary: Mark*. WORDsearch.

Hendriksen, William. 2008. *Baker New Testament Commentary: Exposition of Gospel According to John*. WORDsearch.

—. 2008. *Baker New Testament Commentary: Exposition of the Gospel According to Luke*. WORDsearch.

—. 2008. *Baker New Testament Commentary: Exposition of the Gospel According to Mark*. WORDsearch.

—. 2008. *Baker New Testament Commentary: Exposition of the Gospel According to Matthew*. WORDsearch.

Hindson, Edwardf, James Borland, and Mal Couch. 2010. *Twenty-First Century Biblical Commentary Series: The Gospel of Matthew*. WORDsearch.

Hughes, R. Kent. 2008. *Preaching the Word: John*. WORDsearch.

—. 2008. *Preaching the Word: Luke, Volume I: That You May Know the Truth*. WORDsearch.

—. 2008. *Preaching the Word: Luke, Volume II: That You May Know the Truth*. WORDsearch.

—. 2008. *Preaching the Word: Mark, Volume 11*. WORDsearch.

Johnson, B. W. 2008. *The People's New Testament*. WORDsearch.

Jr., John MacArthur. 2015. *The MacArthur New Testament Commentary: Matthew 1-7.* WORDsearch.

Kaiser, Walter C., Jr., Peter H. Davids, F. F. Bruce, F. F., and Manford T. Brauch. 2004. *Hard Sayings of the Bible.* WORDsearch.

Keener, Greg S. 2006. *The IVP New Testament Commentary Series: Matthew.* WORDsearch.

Kernaghan, Ronald. 2007. *The IVP New Testament Commentary Series: Mark.* WORDsearch.

Larson, Bruce and Lloyd L. Ogilvie. 2015. *The Preacher's Commentary: Luke.* WORDsearch.

Lenski, R.C.H. 2008. *Lenski New Testament Commentary: John.* WORDsearch.

—. 2008. *Lenski New Testament Commentary: Luke.* WORDsearch.

—. 2008. *Lenski New Testament Commentary: Matthew.* WORDsearch.

—. 2008. *Lenski New Testament Commentary: The Interpretation of St. Mark's Gospel.* WORDsearch.

Livingstone Corporation. 2004. *Life Application Bible Commentary: Luke.* WORDsearch.

Livingstone Corporation. 2014. *Life Application Bible Commentary: John.* WORDsearch.

—. 2004. *Life Application Bible Commentary: Mark.* WORDsearch.

MacArthur, John Jr. 2014. *The MacArthur New Testament Commentary: Luke 6-10.* WORDsearch.

MacArthur, John. 2008. *The MacArthur New Testament Commentary: John 12-21.* WORDsearch.

—. 2014. *The MacArthur New Testament Commentary: Luke 11-17.* WORDsearch.

—. 2015. *The MacArthur New Testament Commentary: Mark 9-16.* WORDsearch.

McGowan, James. 2010. *Twenty-First Century Biblical Commentary Series: The Gospel of Mark.* WORDsearch.

McKenna, David L. and Lloyd L. Ogilvie. 2015. *The Preacher's Commentary: Mark.* WORDsearch.

Morris, Leon. 2010. *Pillar New Testament Commentary: The Gospel According to Matthew.* WORDsearch.

O'Donnell, Douglas Sean. 2014. *Preaching the Word: Matthew.* WORDsearch.

Orr, James. 2014. *The International Standard Bible Encyclopaedia.* WORDsearch.

Phillips, John. 2009. *The John Phillips Commentary Series: Exploring the Gospel of John.* WORDsearch.

—. 2009. *The John Phillips Commentary Series: Exploring the Gospel of Luke.* WORDsearch.

—. 2004. *The John Phillips Commentary Series: Exploring the Gospel of Mark.* WORDsearch.

—. 2014. *The John Phillips Commentary Series: Exploring the Gospel of Matthew.* WORDsearch.

Spence, H. D. M. and Joseph Excell. 2008. *The Pulpit Commentary: Volume 17: John.* WORDsearch.

Spence, H. D. M. and Joseph S. Excell. 2008. *The Pulpit Commentary: Volume 16: Mark and Luke.* WORDsearch.

Stein, Robert H. 2013. *New American Commentary: Luke.* WORDsearch.

Towns, Elmer, Mal Couch, and Ed Hindson. 2010. *Twenty-First Century Biblical Commentary Series: The Gospel of John.* WORDsearch.

Webert, Stuart, and Max Anders. 2015. *Holman New Testament Commentary—Matthew.* WORDsearch.

Whitacare, Rodney A. 2014. *The IVP New Testament Commentary Series: John.* WORDsearch.

Wiersbe., Warren W. 2001. *Bible Exposition Commentary (BE Series)—New Testament—vol. 1.* WORDsearch.

Wilkins, Michael J. 2013. *The NIV Application Commentary: Matthew.* WORDsearch.

Zondervan. 2014. *The Expositor's Bible Commentary. Volume 8: Matthew, Mark, Luke.* WORDsearch.